GRAMMAR
CATECHISMS

GRAMMAR CATECHISMS

*Philosophical, Theological,
& Historical Foundations*

THE LOGOS FOUNDATION

LOGOS PRESS PAPERS ◆ λ LOGOS

A DIVISION OF THE LOGOS FOUNDATION

Phoenix, Arizona

Grammar Catechisms: Philosophical, Theological, & Historical Foundations

Copyright © 2023 The Logos Foundation

Logos Papers Press 2023
Phoenix, Arizona
logospaperspress.com
thelogosfoundation.org

Printed in the United States of America

Cover design: Brian J. Phelps
Typesetting: Matthew P. Hicks & Brian J. Phelps
Front cover image: *Meeting by the River* by Robert S. Duncanson, 1864

Library of Congress Cataloging-in-Publication Data pending

The Logos Foundation.
    Grammar catechisms: philosophical, theological, and historical foundations
    Includes bibliographical references and footnotes.
    ISBN 979-8-9880399-5-2 (hardcover)
    ISBN 979-8-9880399-4-5 (paperback)
    ISBN 979-8-9880399-6-9 (e-book)

1. Grammar Catechism 2. Philosophy—Foundation 3. Theology—Foundation 4. Historical Foundation 5. Scripture 6. The Logos Curriculum I. Title

Hear, O Israel: The Lord our God, the Lord is one!
You shall love the Lord your God with all your
heart, with all your soul, and with all your strength.

And these words which I command you today shall
be in your heart. You shall teach them diligently to
your children, and shall talk of them when you sit
in your house, when you walk by the way, when you
lie down, and when you rise up. You shall bind them
as a sign on your hand, and they shall be as front-
lets between your eyes. You shall write them on the
doorposts of your house and on your gates.

—DEUTERONOMY 6:4-9

CONTENTS

GRAMMAR CATECHISMS
IN THEIR ENTIRETY

GRAMMAR CATECHISMS
BY GRADE LEVEL

EDITOR'S PREFACE

THE LOGOS CURRICULUM (TLC) IS A DIVISION OF The Logos Foundation Ministries. **The Logos Foundation**[1] (TLF) is a non-profit 501(c)(3) organization established to promote academic education in Liberal Arts and Theology, in the Church and in the academy. TLF was officially incorporated in 1994 by Dr. Surrendra Gangadean.[2] Dr. Gangadean was also the founding pastor of Westminster Fellowship. He defined the mission for each ministry with the hope of seeing the foundation deepened in the Church, academy, and the culture. His work being completed, Dr. Gangadean went on to glory, February 12, 2022. He left a clear vision for the Logos ministries and prepared those who will now bring the ministries to fruition and ready the next generation of leaders to carry the work forward by bringing educational resources for all ages, from foundation to fullness.

The Logos Foundation Ministries carry out the educational purposes through ten complementary ministries:

---

1. thelogosfoundation.org

2. Dr. Surrendra Gangadean (1943–2022), professor, pastor, husband, father, mentor, friend, and builder, was a giant in the faith, a Philosopher among philosophers, and a Theologian among theologians. He spent a lifetime refining the foundation for philosophy and theology and Historic Christianity. By recognizing the foundation, he was able to name the errors in the history of ideas due to the failure to have laid and built upon that sure foundation. He taught in the college classroom for 45 years, the seminary for over 25 years, and from the pulpit for almost 30 years. He taught Introduction to Philosophy, Logic, Ethics, Philosophy of Religion, Eastern Religions, World Religions, Introduction to Christianity, Introduction to Humanities, Philosophy of Art, The Great Books, Philosophical Theology, Biblical Worldview, Biblical History, Church History, Systematic Theology, Biblical Hermeneutics, and Existential Hermeneutics. In each of his encounters with notable thinkers and with his students, Dr. Gangadean heard, understood, and took intellectual challenges seriously. There was no known basic challenge he did not work through—first for himself, then with others through much discussion, and then in his teaching and writing. He was tenacious in going after a basic dispute or challenge, finding the assumptions underlying the challenge, and then attempting to respond and resolve the problem.

Logos Theological Seminary (LTS) will offer the M.A. degree in Theology, the Master of Divinity (M.Div.), and the Ph.D. in Theology and Philosophy. Currently, LTS assists Westminster Fellowship by preparing the leadership of the church.

Logos College of Liberal Arts (LCLA) will offer the B.A. degree based on a course of studies in the areas of Philosophy, Great Books, Religion, and Humanities (Literature, History, and the Arts).

Logos Preparatory Academy (LPA) uses The Logos Curriculum to provide onsite and online education (K–12) consistent with TLC's Foundational Principles and Objectives.

The Logos Papers[3] (TLP) seeks to make the Logos known through papers covering a broad range of concerns. TLP seeks to articulate the biblical worldview of creation–fall–redemption and its application to culture. TLP seeks to establish the foundation of the biblical worldview from general revelation, special revelation, and Historic Christianity.

---

3. thelogospapers.com

Logos Papers Press[4] (LPP) serves the publishing interests of The Logos Foundation in its various ministries. It makes available in print and digital formats lectures, books, articles, and curricula materials regarding *theological* and *historical foundation.*

 PUBLIC PHILOSOPHY PRESS

Public Philosophy Press[5] (PPP) serves the publishing interests of The Logos Foundation in its various ministries. It makes available in print and digital formats lectures, books, articles, and curricula materials regarding *philosophical foundation* and *humanities.*

Logos Paideia (LP) offers a global community and education online to all who are in the process of discipleship, who wish to lay the foundation and know God through his Word. Paideia is the education of the ideal citizen, and Logos Paideia exists to train citizens of the City of God.

The Logos Curriculum (TLC) is a sequence of courses of study for Logos Preparatory Academy (K–12), Logos College of Liberal Arts, and Logos Theological Seminary. Online, on-site, and homeschool course syllabi are available through Logos Papers Press.

---

4. logospaperspress.com

5. publicphilosophypress.com

Logos Study Center (LSC) hosts extended seminars on selected topics on the three foundations for worldview and culture. It is a place where faculty and students may engage in more intensive critical thinking and dialogue concerning their course of study. It is a place where the moral law and its application to culture may be analyzed and developed. It is a place where the achievements of excellence in the humanities may be more deeply understood and appreciated.

The Logos Archives (TLA) is the collection of handwritten notes, audio and video recordings, and personal library of Surrendra Gangadean. The content of the archives includes sermons, Logos Theological Seminary course lectures, and public lectures. The Surrendra Gangadean Memorial Library is housed at the Logos Study Center.

——

The Logos Curriculum develops material consistent with the distinctives of The Logos Foundation.[6] Understanding these distinctives is necessary to lay a lasting foundation. Foundation is necessary for maturity, fruitfulness, unity, and fullness. Without foundation, there is division and apostasy in the Church, and decay and collapse in the culture. In Scripture, foundation is called for as first principles,[7] for endurance against tempests,[8] for lasting fruit,[9] for unity of the faith and fullness,[10] for a lasting culture in the City of God.[11] Current divisions in the Church and decay in the culture show a longstanding lack of foundation and the need to get to bedrock. Foundation must get to the certainty of clarity, the cornerstone, from which arises inexcusability. It must overcome skepticism and fideism by faith.[12] Failure to achieve

---

6. See p. xvii.

7. *Hebrews 6.*

8. *Matthew 7.*

9. *1 Corinthians 2.*

10. *Ephesians 4.*

11. *Hebrews 11:10; Revelation 21.*

12. *Romans 1:20; Hebrews 11:1.*

comprehensiveness to attain to fullness of life is not new; it has been recurrent throughout history in the collapse of civilizations. A mere return to the past is insufficient for bedrock.

The Logos Curriculum builds upon the distinctives of The Logos Foundation in seeking to overcome the intellectual challenges of our time. Answering the perennial questions in epistemology, metaphysics, ethics, and the humanities requires that we build upon the cumulative insight attained in creation (general revelation as *philosophical foundation*), Scripture (special revelation as *theological foundation*), and providence (Church history as *historical foundation*). Laying foundation demands that the foundational pieces be secure, resting on what is clear—knowledge that is unshakable. A curriculum commensurable to the task of building from foundation to fullness must be: 1) *Presuppositional*—focusing on the more basic to address the less basic—from epistemology to metaphysics to ethics; and from *philosophical* to *theological* to *historical* foundation. 2) *Systematic*—a coherent body of ideas arranged in logical order to provide a framework of interpretation regarding the basic things about God and man, and good and evil. It enables understanding of human nature expressed in worldviews and cultures throughout history. 3) Built upon the *Trivium*—based on the student's intellectual readiness to progress from grammar (memorized factual knowledge) to dialectic (reasoned understanding with justification) to rhetoric (wisdom applied with social virtuosity). And 4) *Interdisciplinary*—the foundational truths regarding God and man, and good and evil are applied to all the disciplines within the humanities (philosophy, theology, history, literature, the arts, and music) with the goal of an integrated way of life leading to fullness in the knowledge of God.

Grammar Catechisms: Philosophical, Theological, and Historical Foundations is the first publication of The Logos Curriculum. The three catechisms constitute a grammatical formulation of learning to be committed to memory from Kindergarten through 4th grade. It can also serve anyone seeking to learn the grammar of the three foundations at any age. The included Core of History and Timeline will be further developed in *A Critical Commentary of World History*—included in the curriculum for the dialectic (5–8 grades) and rhetoric (9–12 grades) levels of learning. In addition, grammar-level clusters of bible verses and Psalms for singing are given for memorization.

The grammar stage allows for four levels: exposure, acquaintance, familiarity, and memorization. In *exposure*, the student is presented with material for the first time. Through increased exposure, the student becomes aware of the content without yet being able to recall it quickly. This constitutes the *acquaintance* level. *Familiarity* entails increased repetition, dozens of times, where the student is comfortable with the material and can recall it fragmentarily, yet is working towards memorization. *Memorization* entails 5–6 years of diligently teaching the material so as to have easy recollection access of its entirety. The content provided in the Catechisms represents the building block for further intellectual growth and maturity with the aim and hope of bearing lasting fruit in the students' lives.

The parent, teacher, or tutor is provided with a list of suggested reading to aid in preparation for understanding the material. Through *Public Philosophy Press* and *Logos Papers Press*, books on the three foundations are being published and additional works will continue to be added.

Philosophical Foundation:

Philosophical Foundation: A Critical Analysis of Basic Beliefs (2022)

History of Philosophy: A Critical Analysis of Unresolved Disputes (2022)

On Natural and Revealed Theology: Collected Essays of Surrendra Gangadean (2023)

Theological Foundation:

Theological Foundation: A Critical Analysis of Christian Belief (2023)

Historical Foundation:

The Westminster Confession of Faith: A Doxological Understanding (2023)

The Westminster Shorter and Larger Catechisms: A Doxological Understanding (2023)

—THE LOGOS FOUNDATION
EDITORIAL BOARD
Phoenix, Arizona
March 2023

DISTINCTIVES OF
THE LOGOS FOUNDATION

1. Clarity and Inexcusability

Foundation begins with the clarity of general revelation concerning God and man and good and evil and the inexcusability of unbelief. This first principle is based on the philosophical foundation of the Principle of Clarity,[1] the theological foundation of Romans 1:20, and the historical foundation of the Westminster Confession of Faith 1.1.

The clarity of general revelation is opposed to skepticism and fideism, both of which, held consistently, lead to nihilism, the loss of all meaning.

What is clear is clear to reason: it is by reason that we understand creation and providence, which reveal God. If we know what is clear, we can show what is clear. Without clarity of general revelation, there is no inexcusability of unbelief, no sin, and therefore no need for Christ and him crucified.

2. Man, the Image of God

Man is the image of God in a manifold sense: in a universal aspect, in regeneration, in one's triune personality, in body/soul unity, in male/female unity, in one's historically conditioned being, and in the uniqueness of one's personhood.

To mankind is given the work of dominion, which is corporate and cumulative, through all of history.

---

1. Surrendra Gangadean, "Paper No. 3: The Principle of Clarity, Rational Presuppositionalism, and Proof," in *The Logos Papers: To Make the Logos Known* (Phoenix: Logos Papers Press, 2022); "Paper No. 53: Common Ground (Part IV): The Principle of Clarity," in *The Logos Papers*.

Man is to name the creation and rule over it. Dominion is exercised through science and technology and humanities and culture. The outcome of dominion is the City of God and the knowledge of God.

3. Man's Chief End

Man's chief end is to glorify God and to enjoy him forever, in all that by which he makes himself known, in all his works of creation and providence.[2] One cannot enjoy God if one does not glorify God. Enjoyment of the creation without glorifying God is not satisfying and leads to all manner of excess.

The chief end of man is the end in itself, the highest good (or simply, the good), which is eternal life, the knowledge of God.[3]

4. The Moral Law

There is a moral law which is clear, comprehensive, and critical. It is clear because it is grounded in human nature and therefore knowable by reason to all men, everywhere, at all times.[4] It is the same in content as the Decalogue, a summary of the moral law, given in Scripture.

The moral law convicts of sin and guides believers in all aspects of life, personal and corporate.

All sin is not a crime. The law given in human nature has a civil aspect and is a source of unity for men and nations.

5. All Have Sinned

All have sinned and come short of the glory of God.[5] Man is fallen: no one seeks God, no one understands, no one is righteous, not even one.[6] The root sin of not seeking and not understanding leads to the fruit sin of all unrighteousness.

---

2. *Shorter Catechism Questions 1, 46, 101; Westminster Confession of Faith 4.1, 5.1.*

3. *John 17:3.*

4. *Deuteronomy 30:12-14; Romans 2:14-15.*

5. *Romans 3:23.*

6. *Romans 3:10-11.*

Sin is an act contrary to one's nature: it is to neglect, avoid, resist, and deny reason, resulting in not acknowledging what is clear about God.

6. Spiritual and Physical Death

The wages of sin is death. This death is spiritual, not physical, and is inherent in sin. It is meaninglessness, boredom, and guilt, without end.[7]

Original creation was very good: natural evil (which leads to physical death) is due to moral evil (sin). Natural evil was imposed by God as the third and final call back from moral evil and spiritual death.[8]

Natural evil of toil and strife, and old age, sickness, and physical death serves to restrain, recall from, and remove moral evil. Natural evil increases, as moral evil increases, and becomes war, famine, and plague.

The call back of the curse is given with the promise of redemption. Through a spiritual war which is age-long and agonizing, good will overcome evil.[9]

7. Christ the Redeemer

Jesus Christ comes in the place of Adam to undo what Adam did and to do what Adam failed to do. Christ is the Lamb of God who takes away the sin of the world.[10] Christ is the eternal Word of God (the Logos) incarnate who makes God known.[11]

The life of the Logos is the light of reason in all men.[12] The Logos is revealed in all his works of creation and history.[13] The Logos comes to the people of God in history as Scripture.[14] The Logos, rejected as

---

7. *John 11:25-26; Ephesians 2:1; Revelation 20:6.*

8. *Genesis 3:7-19.*

9. *Genesis 3:15; 2 Corinthians 10:4-5; Revelation 19:11-21.*

10. *John 1:29.*

11. *John 1:1, 14.*

12. *John 1:4.*

13. *John 1:10.*

14. *John 1:11.*

reason and as revelation in creation and Scripture, becomes incarnate to take away sin and to make God known.[15]

8. The Historic Christian Faith

Christ sends the Holy Spirit to lead the Church into all truth.[16] This comes through the work of the pastor-teachers,[17] who, in response to challenges, after much discussion, come to agreement expressed in confessions and creeds, for the unity of the faith.[18]

Failure to build on the Historic Christian Faith has divided the body of Christ. Challenges since the Reformation (1650) still require response. Without the Church's response, human cultures decay and perish.

The Holy Spirit leads believers personally into the truth by regeneration and sanctification.

9. The Church

The Church is the body of Christ and is the pillar and ground of the truth. It is the salt of the earth and the light of the world.[19]

The Church is for worship and discipleship. It is to worship God in spirit and in truth. Only the Psalms given for singing in the corporate worship of God preserves pure and entire the biblical worldview of creation, fall, and redemption.

Discipleship is for sanctification, which is by knowing the truth. The Word of God (the Logos) is truth. Knowing the truth in its fullness makes a person free.[20]

---

15. *John 1:14.*
16. *John 16:13.*
17. *Ephesians 4:11-16.*
18. *Acts 15.*
19. *1 Timothy 3:15; Matthew 5:13-14.*
20. *John 17:17; 8:32.*

10. Hope

The Sabbath affirms the hope that Christ, through the Church, will subdue all things unto himself, and then the end of history will come.[21] The resurrection comes as the last act of dominion and completes it.

There is no rapture before the resurrection of all men at the end of history.[22]

There is no direct knowledge of God (no beatific vision) apart from God's self-revelation in his Word given in all of creation and providence, which includes Scripture.

By the rule of Christ, the earth shall be full of the knowledge of the Lord as the waters cover the sea.[23]

---

21. *Genesis 2:1-3; Exodus 20:8; 1 Corinthians 15:25-26; John 20:1-18.*

22. *John 5:28-29; 1 Thessalonians 4:15-17.*

23. *Isaiah 11:9.*

THE LOGOS CURRICULUM
Foundational Principles

M AN'S CHIEF END IS TO GLORIFY GOD, in all that by which he makes himself known, in all his works of creation and providence. The lasting joy of eternal life comes from knowing God.[1]

Man is made in the image of God, to know God through the work of dominion, to fill the earth with the knowledge of God as the waters cover the sea. In dominion, man is to name the creation, which reveals God's glory, and to rule over it: in the realm of nature—under natural law, through science and technology; in the human realm—under the moral law, through the humanities and culture.[2]

The Logos Curriculum (TLC) incorporates the classical Trivium: grammar (K–4), dialectic (5–8), and rhetoric (9–12). The Trivium is based on the student's intellectual readiness to progress from fact-based knowledge, to reasoned understanding, to wisdom in applying what has been learned to oneself and to the world.

TLC is first *preparatory*, for further academic study and for life-long learning. TLC emphasizes *critical thinking*, applying reason to critically examine assumptions and presuppositions for meaning. TLC understands particular beliefs, values, and actions as integral parts of a person's *worldview* built more or less coherently upon a set of basic philosophical assumptions. And last, TLC seeks to appreciate the highest achievements of all of human culture, manifest, in part, in the *Great Books Tradition*.

TLC builds upon a scope and sequence of core knowledge needed at each grade level. Layers of enrichment are added to the core. TLC

---

1. *SCQ. 1, 101; WCF 4.1, 5.1; John 17:3.*
2. *Genesis 1; Isaiah 11:9.*

offers layers of assistance for parents and students in implementing the curriculum.

The Humanities answers the question "What is Man?" by examining man's view of himself in the varying worldviews and cultures. The Humanities consists of Philosophy, Theology, History, Literature, the Arts, and Music. History focuses attention on the age-long and agonizing conflict between good and evil, between truth and falsehood, in every aspect of human existence, in the hope that only what retains meaning will last.

The Logos Curriculum seeks to recover, to advance, and to secure the highest achievements of civilization built upon the Logos, the eternal Word of God, who makes God fully known.[3]

---

3. *John 1:1, 4-5, 10, 11, 14; 16:12-13; 3:3; 8:31-32; 17:17.*

THE LOGOS CURRICULUM
Objectives

T HE LOGOS CURRICULUM IS BASED ON THE LOGOS which makes God known.[1] The good, which is the knowledge of God, is for all men, everywhere, at all times. The Logos Curriculum for the Academy (K–12) is guided by the following objectives: College Preparatory, Critical Thinking, Worldview Focus, and Great Books Tradition.

The Logos Curriculum may be used in a variety of formats which can be combined: online, on-site, and home school.

The pedagogy reflects the insight of the Trivium, knowledge of scope and sequence, and established learning practices compatible with the objectives and goals of The Logos Curriculum.

College Preparatory is for a Liberal Arts education.

The Truth sets us free.[2] The Logos is Truth.[3] We are made free to be fully human, beyond the boundaries of personal, parochial traditions, to love God with the whole heart. Through study of the Humanities, we are made aware of the universals of the whole range of the human condition. A Liberal Arts education is for the good, the highest value, beyond the virtues. It is for life, beyond a livelihood. It is lifelong education.

---

1. *John 1:1-18.*
2. *John 8:32.*
3. *John 17:17.*

Critical Thinking is for knowledge.

Knowledge is based on Common Ground[4] which makes thought and discourse possible. Knowledge assumes the Principle of Clarity over and against skepticism and fideism. Critical thinking overcomes objections to knowledge based on uncritically held assumptions. Critical thinking enables us to find meaning and to settle disputes.

Worldview Focus seeks meaning through integration.

The Logos Curriculum seeks to understand the context of human choice in an integrated vision of life. It seeks to understand the structure and challenges present in every worldview. It seeks to understand how a worldview comes to expression in a culture. It seeks to understand how human life and cultures flourish through integrity.

The Great Books Tradition affirms historically cumulative insight.

The Logos Curriculum is based on what is classical, achievements of enduring value. The Great Tradition is based on the long-standing, on-going discussion. It is based on judgment that is well-informed and well-instructed. It is based on achievement from all cultures, revealing the human aspiration for excellence.

---

4. Gangadean, "Paper No. 2: Common Ground: The Necessary Condition for Thought and Discourse," in *The Logos Papers*; See also Papers No. 50–53: Common Ground (Parts I–IV) in *The Logos Papers*.

GRAMMAR CATECHISMS
IN THEIR ENTIRETY

PHILOSOPHICAL FOUNDATION GRAMMAR

General Revelation

EPISTEMOLOGY

1. What is epistemology?

Epistemology answers the question: how do we know?

2. How do we have knowledge?

We know by reason and argument.

3. What is reason in itself?

Reason in itself is the laws of thought.

4. What are the three laws of thought?

The laws of thought are: the law of identity, the law of non-contradiction, and the law of excluded middle.

5. What is reason in its use?

Reason in its use is formative, critical, interpretive, and constructive.

6. What are the three forms of thought resulting from the three acts of reason?

We use reason to form concepts, judgments, and arguments.

7. What is a concept?

In a concept, the mind grasps the essential nature of a being, class of beings, or aspect of beings.

8. What is an essence?

An essence is the set of qualities that all members of a class and only members always have, and distinguishes them from all non-members.

9. How is a concept expressed?

A concept is expressed by a term; a term is a word or group of words.

10. What is a judgment?

In a judgment, the mind relates two concepts by affirmation or negation.

11. How is a judgment expressed?

A judgment is expressed in a statement.

12. What is an argument?

In an argument, premises are given as reasons to support a conclusion.

13. What is a valid argument?

An argument is valid if the premises logically support the conclusion.

14. What is a sound argument?

An argument is sound if it is valid and its premises are true.

15. How is reason used critically?

Reason is used critically as a test for meaning.

16. How is reason used to interpret?

Reason is used to interpret (or give meaning to) experience in light of one's basic beliefs.

17. How is reason used constructively?

Reason is used to construct a coherent world and life view.

18. What is reason in us?

Reason in us is natural, ontological, transcendental, and fundamental.

19. How is reason natural?

Reason is universal; it is the same in all persons at all times.

20. How is reason ontological?

Reason applies to being as well as thought.

21. How is reason transcendental?

Reason is self-attesting and the highest authority.

22. How is reason fundamental?

Reason is basic to other aspects of human personality.

23. What is our presupposition?

Our presupposition is our set of basic beliefs used to give meaning to our experience.

24. What are the three areas and questions in each set of basic beliefs?

Epistemology—how do we know?; Metaphysics—what is real?; Ethics—what ought I to do?

25. What is the basic pair of beliefs in epistemology?

The basic pair of beliefs in epistemology is: knowledge is possible, that is, some things are clear vs. knowledge is not possible and basic things are not clear.

26. What is the basic pair of beliefs in metaphysics?

The basic pair of beliefs in metaphysics is: only some is eternal (God) vs. all is eternal (in some form or other).

27. What is the basic pair of beliefs in ethics?

The basic pair of beliefs in ethics is: the good is the end in itself vs. the good is virtue or happiness.

28. Who holds to which of the basic beliefs?

We are more or less conscious and consistent in our basic beliefs; each person holds an admixture of both; there is a conflict of unbelief in the believer and belief in the unbeliever.

29. What should be our response to this conflict?

Our response should be to be more conscious and consistent in our basic beliefs.

30. How does history relate to this conflict?

History is an outworking of this conflict in each person and between all persons.

31. What will be the outcome of this conflict?

Only what retains meaning can last; meaning will overcome meaninglessness; light will overcome darkness; good will overcome evil.

METAPHYSICS

32. What is metaphysics?

Metaphysics answers the question: what is real or eternal?

33. What is our most basic concept?

Our most basic concept is eternal existence.

34. What is meant by eternal?

Eternal means what has always existed and will always exist.

35. What are the most basic answers to the question: what is eternal?

Either all is eternal, or none is eternal, or only some is eternal.

36. What kinds of things exist?

What exists is either matter or spirit.

37. What are the essential qualities of matter?

Matter in itself is non-living; it has size in space, but no consciousness.

38. What are the essential qualities of spirit?

Spirit has no size, but it is conscious.

39. Who believes all is eternal?

Material monists, spiritual monists, and dualists believe all is eternal.

40. What is material monism?

Material monism is the belief that all is matter and matter is eternal.

41. What is spiritual monism?

Spiritual monism is the belief that all is spirit and spirit is eternal.

42. What is dualism?

Dualism is the belief that both matter and spirit exist and both matter and spirit are eternal.

43. Who believes only some is eternal?

Theists and deists believe only God is eternal.

44. What is the difference between theists and deists?

Theists believe God created and rules; deists believe God created but does not rule.

45. Who believes none is eternal?

Buddhism teaches that all is *dukkha*, that only change or process is real.

46. Must there be something eternal?

If nothing is eternal, then being must have come into existence from non-being, which is impossible.

47. Is matter eternal?

If matter were eternal, it would be self-maintaining, but matter is not self-maintaining.

48. Is everything made of matter?

The mind is not the brain; matter cannot explain human thinking or seeing.

49. Is the soul eternal?

If the soul (or mind) were eternal, it would know everything, but we do not know everything, so the soul is not eternal.

50. Does the material world exist?

The cause of what I see is not my mind or another mind, but outside all minds.

51. Can there be only one mind and its ideas?

The world cannot be an illusion (*maya*) in the one mind which knows everything.

52. Are we all part of one mind (God)?

We cannot be infinite and eternal or finite and eternal.

53. Why did God create?

God created because he is, and he reveals his glory by creation.

54. Who made God?

There must be something eternal, and only God is eternal.

55. What is God?

God is a spirit who is infinite, eternal, and unchangeable, in his power and wisdom.

56. Is God good?

God created man with a concern for goodness; therefore, God is good.

57. What is moral evil?

Moral evil is an act contrary to one's nature as a rational being; it is to neglect, avoid, resist, and deny (NARD) reason.

58. What is natural evil?

Natural evil is suffering due to external circumstance; it is toil and strife, and old age, sickness, and death.

59. Did God create the world good?

Because God is all good and all-powerful, he could, would, must, and did create the world without any evil.

60. Why is there moral evil?

Moral evil serves to deepen the revelation of God's glory.

61. What is the inherent consequence of moral evil?

The inherent consequence of moral evil is meaninglessness, boredom, and guilt.

62. Why is there natural evil?

Natural evil is imposed by God to restrain, recall from, and remove moral evil; it is a call to stop and think.

63. Will natural evil be removed?

Natural evil will be removed when moral evil is removed.

64. Will moral evil be removed?

Moral evil is gradually removed as unbelief in every form is overcome by belief.

65. How can God be both just and merciful to man in moral evil?

Special revelation is required to know how God can be both just and merciful.

66. Does special revelation exist?

Special revelation exists if it is consistent with clear general revelation and shows how God is both just and merciful.

ETHICS

67. What is ethics?

Ethics answers the question: what is the good?

68. At the most basic level, what is the good?
The good is the end in itself; it is sought for its own sake; it is the highest value.

69. What is virtue?
Virtue is a means to the good; virtue is not the good.

70. What are the three kinds of virtue?
The three kinds of virtue are moral, natural, and instrumental.

71. What is happiness?
Happiness is the effect of possessing what one believes is the good; happiness is not the good.

72. What is lasting happiness?
Lasting happiness is the effect of possessing what is truly the good.

73. What is the means to the good?
The means to the good is the moral law through the work of dominion.

74. What is the good for a being?
The good for a being is according to the nature of that being.

75. What is the good for man?
The good for man as a rational being is the use of reason to the fullest; reason is used to understand the nature of things; the nature of things created reveals the nature of God; the good for man is the knowledge of God.

76. What are the 10 formal characteristics of the good?
The good is continuing, inexhaustible, comprehensive, inalienable, corporate, cumulative, communal, fulfilling, ultimate, and transformative.

77. How is the good the source of unity?
The good is given in human nature, which is one and the same for all; therefore, it is the source of unity in each person and among all persons.

78. What are the three most basic characteristics of the moral law?

The moral law is clear, comprehensive, and critical.

79. How is the moral law clear?

The moral law is given in human nature, which is easily knowable by all human beings.

80. How is the moral law comprehensive?

The moral law guides all choices that express all aspects of human nature.

81. How is the moral law critical?

The moral law has inherent consequences of spiritual life or death.

82. What is moral law 1 about?

Moral law 1 is about the good and the real.

83. How is moral law 1 given in human nature?

By nature, we make choices concerning means and ends; the end in itself is the good, which is grounded in what is eternal.

84. What is moral law 2 about?

Moral law 2 is about the nature of thinking and the divine nature.

85. How is moral law 2 given in human nature?

By nature, we think, and thinking by nature is presuppositional; we must think of the finite (man) in light of the infinite (God).

86. What is moral law 3 about?

Moral law 3 is about unity and integrity.

87. How is moral law 3 given in human nature?

Human nature is one, which is a natural unity; to be undivided we must be concerned for consistency.

88. What is moral law 4 about?

Moral law 4 is about work and rest.

89. How is moral law 4 given in human nature?

By nature, the work of dominion is necessary to achieve the good; when the good is achieved, work will cease.

90. What is moral law 5 about?

Moral law 5 is about authority and insight.

91. How is moral law 5 given in human nature?

By nature, we are born ignorant, and by nature, we need teaching based on insight into the good and the means to the good.

92. What is moral law 6 about?

Moral law 6 is about human dignity and rationality.

93. How is moral law 6 given in human nature?

We are born human, with a capacity to understand that distinguishes man from animal.

94. What is moral law 7 about?

Moral law 7 is about spiritual fidelity and infidelity.

95. How is moral law 7 given in human nature?

We are born of a sexual union between one man and one woman; ordinary fidelity is based on fidelity to the good.

96. What is moral law 8 about?

Moral law 8 is about talent and value.

97. How is moral law 8 given in human nature?

We are each born with some talent; by talent, we achieve some aspect of the good.

98. What is moral law 9 about?

Moral law 9 is about truth and justice.

99. How is moral law 9 given in human nature?

We are born equal and, in justice, equals are treated equally; truth is necessary and sufficient for justice.

100. What is moral law 10 about?

Moral law 10 is about contentment and the good.

101. How is moral law 10 given in human nature?

We are born changeable in our understanding; discontent arises from a misunderstanding of good and evil.

102. What is the work of dominion?

The work of dominion is given to man, made in the image of God, and consists in naming and ruling the creation.

103. How does man name and rule in the natural world and in the human world?

Man names and rules in the natural world by science and technology, and in the human world by the humanities and the arts.

104. Given moral and natural evil in the world, how can the work of dominion be accomplished?

Under creation–fall–redemption, Christ, in the place of Adam, will undo what Adam did, and will do what Adam failed to do by subduing all things to himself.

105. How does Christ subdue all things to himself?

Christ subdues all things by making disciples of all nations, teaching them to observe all he commands, and so brings mankind from the Garden of Eden to the City of God.

106. What is the two-fold outcome of the completed work of Christ?

The outcome of Christ's work is that every thought raised up against the knowledge of God will be taken captive, and the earth will be full of the knowledge of the Lord as the waters cover the sea.

THEOLOGICAL FOUNDATION

GRAMMAR

Special Revelation: Genesis 1–3

INTRODUCTION

1. What are the seven senses of the Word of God?

The Word of God (the Logos) 1) is eternal—the Son of God, 2) is in all men as reason, 3) is in creation as clear general revelation, 4) is in history as special revelation (Scripture), 5) is incarnate in Jesus Christ, 6) is in the Church, by the Holy Spirit, as the Historic Christian Faith, and 7) is in each believer by regeneration and sanctification.

2. What is general revelation?

General revelation is what can be known of God from the creation; it can be known by all men, everywhere, at all times.

3. What is special revelation?

Special revelation is what can be known of God from Scripture; Scripture is given by God for the redemption of man.

4. What does Scripture as redemptive revelation assume?

Scripture assumes the reality of sin in the rejection of the Word of God in man as reason and in the creation as clear general revelation.

5. Why is Scripture necessary?

Scripture is necessary to show how God is both just and merciful to man in sin.

6. How does Scripture show God is both just and merciful to man in sin?

Scripture focuses on the person and work of Christ, the Word of God incarnate, who restores mankind to life in the knowledge of God.

7. What is assumed in reading and understanding Scripture?

The use of reason and knowledge of clear general revelation are assumed in reading and understanding Scripture.

8. What is meant in saying Scripture is organic?

Scripture is a unity that grows; from the beginning, the foundation of Scripture is given in organic seed form.

9. What is Foundation (Philosophical, Theological, and Historical) necessary for?

Foundation is necessary to go on to maturity, fruitfulness, unity of the faith, and fullness of the knowledge of God (Ephesians 4; Hebrews 6).

10. Where is Theological Foundation given in Scripture?

Theological Foundation is given in Genesis 1–3.

11. What is meant in saying Genesis 1–3 is Theological Foundation?

Scripture builds on, is to be understood by, and is the development of what is revealed in Genesis 1–3; understanding the beginning is necessary for understanding all that follows.

12. What are the three basic themes of Theological Foundation?

The three basic themes of Theological Foundation are: Creation, Fall, and Redemption.

CREATION

13. What is the first point of Creation?

Creation is revelation: necessarily, intentionally, and exclusively.

14. What general principle is to be understood from *creation is revelation*?

The visible reveals the invisible; the physical reveals the spiritual; the creation reveals the Creator.

15. How is creation revelation necessarily?

The act of a being reveals the nature of that being; the acts of God in creation and providence reveal the nature of God.

16. How is creation revelation intentionally?

Creation was very good; it was what God intended; God intends to be known through his acts.

17. How is creation revelation exclusively?

There is no revelation of God apart from his works of creation and providence.

18. What are the two types of creation?

The two types of creation are original and subsequent creation.

19. What is original creation?

Original creation is *ex nihilo*.

20. What is meant by creation *ex nihilo*?

God brought the substance of creation into being out of nothing; there was no pre-existent material.

21. What does creation *ex nihilo* reveal about God?

Creation *ex nihilo* reveals that only God the Creator is infinite, eternal, and unchangeable.

22. When did time begin?

Time began with the beginning of creation.

23. What new work of God begins upon creation *ex nihilo*?

Upon creation, God begins his work of providence: the Spirit of God moves upon the face of the waters.

24. What is subsequent creation?

Subsequent creation is God forming and filling the cosmos after original creation.

25. What is the second point of Creation?

The revelation is full and clear.

26. In general, how is the revelation full?

The whole earth is full of his glory (Isaiah 6:3); everything in creation and providence reveals God's glory.

27. What is special creation?

Special creation is God directly creating each kind of living creature.

28. Specifically, how is the revelation full?

The vast array of the creation, each after its kind, and the multitudes of human beings in history are a full revelation of God's glory.

29. How are we given a full revelation of God's justice and mercy?

A full revelation of God's justice and mercy is given in providence of the Fall and of redemption.

30. How is the revelation clear?

God's eternal power and divine nature are clearly revealed in the things that are made (Romans 1:20); the law of God is written on the hearts of all men (Romans 2:14-15).

31. Are all men responsible to know this clear revelation?

The clarity of general revelation makes the unbelief of mankind without excuse.

32. How was man created?

Man was created in the image of God, male and female.

33. What is meant by man is the image of God?

Man is finite, temporal, and changeable in his being, wisdom, power, holiness, justice, goodness, and truth.

34. What are male and female?

Male and female are both aspects of the image of God; they are spiritual characteristics in God, and come from God.

35. What is the third point of Creation?

Eternal life is knowing God (John 17:3).

36. What is meant by eternal life?

Our knowledge of God begins in this life and grows unendingly in the next life.

37. How is eternal life referred to in general revelation (Philosophical Foundation)?

From general revelation, the good is the knowledge of God.

38. How is eternal life referred to in Historic Christianity (Historical Foundation)?

From Historic Christianity, man's chief end is to glorify God and to enjoy him forever.

39. What does it mean to glorify God?

To glorify God is to know his glory and to make his glory known.

40. What is the fourth point of Creation?

The knowledge of God is through the work of dominion.

41. How did God bless man in relation to the work of dominion?

God blessed man to be fruitful and multiply, to fill the earth and subdue it and to rule over it.

42. What two aspects are included in the call to dominion?

In dominion, man is called to name the creation and to rule over it.

43. How does man name the creation?

Man names the creation in grasping the nature of all beings in all their parts and relations.

44. When does naming the creation begin and end?

God begins naming in his work of creation, and man as the image of God continues until everything is named.

45. How does man rule over the creation?

Man rules over the creation by developing the powers latent in himself and in the creation so as to make known the glory of God.

46. How is the work of dominion to be achieved?

The work of dominion is to be achieved by all of mankind working together through all of history.

47. What is the fifth point of Creation?

The earth shall be full of the knowledge of the Lord as the waters cover the sea (Isaiah 11:9).

48. How does God signify that his work of creation is complete?

God signifies that his work of creation is complete by blessing the seventh day and calling it holy—the Sabbath day.

49. What does the Sabbath signify for man as the image of God?

As God completed the work of creation, so man will complete the work of dominion.

50. Why is the Sabbath to be observed by all men?

The Sabbath is a perpetual reminder to man of his origin, destiny, and hope.

51. What was the condition of original creation?

Original creation was very good; there was no moral or natural evil; animals were given the green vegetation for food, and humans did not die.

FALL

52. What is the first point of the Fall?

The covenant of creation: representation, probation, and manifestation; the covenant of marriage.

53. Where is the covenant of creation given in Scripture?

The covenant of creation is given in Genesis 2.

54. What is the purpose of the covenant of creation?

It is the purpose of the LORD God to establish mankind in a permanent relationship with himself.

55. What is meant by mankind being established in a permanent relationship with the LORD?

The LORD's gracious purpose is to bring man from a state in which he could fall away in sin, to a state in which he is established in righteousness.

56. How is the doctrine of covenant representation revealed in general?

The Garden of Eden is the biological, geographical, and historical center of life on earth; all life flows out from this center.

57. What is visibly represented by the two trees at the center of all life in Eden?

All of life is centered in man's choice between two ways: good and evil, life and death.

58. How is the doctrine of covenant representation revealed particularly?

As covenant head of the human race, Adam represents the entire human race; the act of one man will affect all.

59. What is meant by probation in the covenant of creation?
Adam is to be tested concerning his pursuit of God's purpose for mankind: the knowledge of God through the work of dominion.

60. What is meant by manifestation in the covenant of creation?
The inward, invisible choice of good and evil is manifested in the outward act of obedience regarding eating from the two trees.

61. What does the visible covenant of marriage reveal?
The visible covenant of marriage between man and woman reveals the invisible covenant of creation between God and man.

62. In what moral state was man created?
Man was created in a state of moral innocence and purity; they felt no shame in either their inward or outward condition.

63. What is the second point of the Fall?
Temptation: the purpose, the agent, and the argument.

64. What is the purpose of the temptation?
The temptation is a test of one's faith or understanding of good and evil; it serves to reveal the inward condition of man, whether he has been seeking the knowledge of God as the good.

65. What purpose does the agent of temptation serve?
Neither the agent nor the temptation is the cause of sin, but rather the outward occasion that reveals sin.

66. In what form does the test of temptation come?
The temptation comes in the form of an argument addressed to the understanding.

67. What two parts of the argument can be identified?
A reason or premise ("for you shall be like God knowing good and evil") is given to support the conclusion ("you shall not surely die").

68. In saying, "you shall not surely die," what is the tempter denying?

The tempter, who is the devil, denies the Word of God regarding the inherent consequence of spiritual death for disobeying God's command.

69. In saying, "for you shall be like God knowing good and evil," what is the tempter offering?

The tempter offers the impossible promise of man becoming like God in how he knows good and evil.

70. Why is the promise of man becoming like God in knowing good and evil impossible?

God as the infinite Creator knows good and evil by determining it in the act of creating; man as a finite creature knows good and evil by discovering it according to God's creation.

71. What inward reality is revealed in the outward act of eating from the tree of the knowledge of good and evil?

Man had ceased seeking to know God and so failed to understand the clear difference between God the Creator and man the creature with respect to knowing good and evil; instead, man had put himself in the place of God to determine good and evil.

72. What is the third point of the Fall?

Sin: not seeking, not understanding, and not doing what is right.

73. What was the immediate cause of man's disobedience in eating the forbidden fruit?

Man put the desire for beauty, pleasure, and wisdom apart from God above the love of God.

74. What does the account of the Fall of man particularly reveal?

The account of the Fall of man particularly reveals original sin.

75. What is meant by original sin?

Original sin is the first sin in the history of mankind, and it is how sin at its root originates in all.

76. What is meant by root sin and fruit sin?

The root sin of not seeking and not understanding leads to the fruit sin of not doing what is right.

77. What is the fourth point of the Fall?

Death: two kinds of death: physical and spiritual; the wages of sin is spiritual death.

78. In general, what is spiritual death?

Spiritual death is the inherent consequence of sin; it is present and inherent in sin, not future and imposed.

79. Inwardly, what is spiritual death?

Inwardly, spiritual death is meaninglessness, boredom, and guilt, increasing without end.

80. Outwardly, what is spiritual death?

Outwardly, spiritual death is the breakdown and reversal of the order established by creation.

81. How does physical death reveal spiritual death?

Physical death is imposed by God as a call back from spiritual death.

82. What is the fifth point of the Fall?

Theodicy: why is there evil? Evil deepens the divine revelation.

83. How does evil deepen the divine revelation?

The revelation of the divine justice and mercy particularly is deepened.

84. How is the divine justice deepened in permitting evil?

Justice is revealed in the connection between sin and death; moral evil as unbelief is allowed to work itself out in world history in every form and degree of admixture with belief.

85. How is the divine mercy deepened in imposing natural evil?

Mercy is revealed in redemption; natural evil is imposed by God to restrain, recall from, and remove moral evil; as a call back, natural evil requires redemptive revelation to show how God is both just and merciful, at the same time, to man in sin.

86. How is moral evil being removed?

Moral evil is removed gradually; if it is removed abruptly, then the revelation will not be deepened; if it is not removed, then the revelation will not be seen.

REDEMPTION

87. What is the first point of Redemption?

The first call back to repentance: shame (inward/conscience). The first response: self-deception (cover up).

88. What was the immediate effect of the loss of righteousness through disobedience?

The immediate effect of the loss of righteousness through disobedience was that they realized their spiritual nakedness, now manifest in their visible nakedness, and felt ashamed.

89. How does the visible reveal the invisible in the state of sin?

Under sin, physical nakedness is a reminder of spiritual nakedness.

90. What was the outward response to the shame of nakedness?

Shame is avoided by making a covering of leaves, yet the covering is still seen and still reminds.

91. What was the inward response to the shame of nakedness?

By self-deception, one avoids acknowledging the sin of not seeking and not understanding what is clear about God.

92. What is the second point of Redemption?

The second call back: self-examination (outward/the question: where are you?). The second response: self-justification (blaming others).

93. How does the second call back go beyond the first call back?

The second call back is outer and from another (God) vs. inward and from within oneself.

94. In asking, "Where are you?" what is God calling for?

In asking, "Where are you?" God, who is all-knowing, is calling man to examine himself.

95. In asking, "Have you eaten from the tree of which I commanded you . . .?" what is God calling for?

In asking, "Have you eaten from the tree of which I commanded you...?" God is calling man who is hiding in guilt and fear to confess his sin.

96. How does man seek to justify himself in response to the second call back?

Man seeks to justify himself by blaming others, both the woman and God, for his own act of disobedience.

97. Instead of seeking to justify himself, what should man have seen?

Man, in sin, cannot justify himself before God; he must rely only on God's mercy.

98. What is the third point of Redemption?

The third call back: the promise and the curse. The third response: repentance and faith (Adam names his wife Eve).

99. How does the third call back go beyond the second call back?

The third call back is given in deed, beyond word; it is the final and lasting call back.

100. What is the promise?

The promise is that through a spiritual war, which is age-long and agonizing, good will overcome evil.

101. What will the seed of the woman (the Second Adam—Christ) do in place of the first Adam?

The seed of the woman will undo what Adam did (by paying the penalty for sin) and do what Adam failed to do (by filling the earth with the knowledge of God through the work of dominion).

102. What is the curse?

The curse consists of toil and strife, and old age, sickness, and death.

103. At times, how is the curse intensified corporately?

The curse is intensified corporately to war, famine, and plague.

104. Why is the curse to be understood as the mercy of God and not punishment (justice)?

The curse is merciful in that it is imposed by God as the final, continuing call back from sin and self-deception and self-justification; the curse is not punishment, which is inherent in sin.

105. How is the curse to be understood in relation to covenant representation?

The curse is imposed by God on all mankind as a call back from sin through Adam's representation.

106. When will the curse (or natural evil) be removed?

The curse will be removed when sin (or moral evil) is removed and there is no more natural evil as a call to repentance.

107. What response is given by man to the promise and curse?

Man chooses to obey in repentance by accepting life for mankind under the curse, with faith and hope in the promise of redemption.

108. What is the fourth point of Redemption?

Justification: forgiveness of sin through the death of another (the coats of skin).

109. What is God's first response to man's faith in his promise?

God justifies man by covering his guilt through vicarious atonement—through the sacrifice of another in the place of Adam; man is given the garment of skin to cover his nakedness.

110. Under covenant representation, what is triple imputation?

Adam's guilt is imputed to all whom he represents; the guilt of all who accept the promise is imputed to the one promised in the place of Adam; the righteousness of the one sacrificed is imputed to all who believe.

111. What is the fifth point of Redemption?

Sanctification: cleansing from sin through suffering (the expulsion).

112. What is God's second response to man's faith?

God expels man from the Garden, to live under the effects of the curse, to be sanctified (cleansed) from sin and self-deception and self-justification.

113. By what means is man sanctified?

Sanctification is by knowledge of the truth; this knowledge comes through suffering under the curse.

114. Why can the call back through the curse not be avoided?

There is no life apart from the knowledge of God, and under sin, there is no knowledge of God apart from suffering in the work of dominion; the way to the tree of life is guarded, and all born of Adam must die physically.

115. For those who are justified, when is sanctification complete?

Sanctification for those who are justified continues until death; it is incomplete until death and ends with death.

HISTORICAL FOUNDATION
GRAMMAR

Historic Christianity:
The Westminster Shorter Catechism

MAN'S CHIEF END AND
THE WORD OF GOD

1. What is the chief end of man?

Man's chief end is to glorify God, and to enjoy him forever.

2. What rule has God given to direct us how we may glorify and enjoy him?

The Word of God, which is contained in the Scriptures of the Old and New Testaments, is the only rule to direct us how we may glorify and enjoy him.

3. What do the Scriptures principally teach?

The Scriptures principally teach what man is to believe concerning God, and what duty God requires of man.

GOD AND HIS DECREES

4. What is God?

God is a spirit, infinite, eternal, and unchangeable, in his being, wisdom, power, holiness, justice, goodness, and truth.

5. Are there more Gods than one?

There is but one only, the living and true God.

6. How many persons are there in the Godhead?

There are three persons in the Godhead; the Father, the Son, and the Holy Ghost; and these three are one God, the same in substance, equal in power and glory.

7. What are the decrees of God?

The decrees of God are his eternal purpose, according to the counsel of his will, whereby, for his own glory, he has foreordained whatsoever comes to pass.

8. How does God execute his decrees?

God executes his decrees in the works of creation and providence.

CREATION AND PROVIDENCE

9. What is the work of creation?

The work of creation is God's making all things of nothing, by the word of his power, in the space of six days, and all very good.

10. How did God create man?

God created man male and female, after his own image, in knowledge, righteousness, and holiness, with dominion over the creatures.

11. What are God's works of providence?

God's works of providence are his most holy, wise, and powerful preserving and governing all his creatures, and all their actions.

12. What special act of providence did God exercise toward man in the estate wherein he was created?

When God had created man, he entered into a covenant of life with him, upon condition of perfect obedience; forbidding him to eat of the tree of the knowledge of good and evil, upon the pain of death.

THE FALL OF MAN

13. Did our first parents continue in the estate wherein they were created?

Our first parents, being left to the freedom of their own will, fell from the estate wherein they were created, by sinning against God.

14. What is sin?

Sin is any want of conformity unto, or transgression of, the law of God.

15. What was the sin whereby our first parents fell from the estate wherein they were created?

The sin whereby our first parents fell from the estate wherein they were created was their eating the forbidden fruit.

16. Did all mankind fall in Adam's first transgression?

The covenant being made with Adam, not only for himself, but for his posterity; all mankind, descending from him by ordinary generation, sinned in him, and fell with him, in his first transgression.

17. Into what estate did the fall bring mankind?

The fall brought mankind into an estate of sin and misery.

18. Wherein consists the sinfulness of that estate whereinto man fell?

The sinfulness of that estate whereinto man fell consists in the guilt of Adam's first sin, the want of original righteousness, and the corruption of his whole nature, which is commonly called original sin; together with all actual transgressions which proceed from it.

19. What is the misery of that estate whereinto man fell?

All mankind by their fall lost communion with God, are under his wrath and curse, and so made liable to all miseries in this life, to death itself, and to the pains of hell forever.

THE COVENANT OF GRACE AND
THE PERSON AND WORK OF CHRIST

20. Did God leave all mankind to perish in the estate of sin and misery?

God having, out of his mere good pleasure, from all eternity, elected some to everlasting life, did enter into a covenant of grace, to deliver them out of the estate of sin and misery, and to bring them into an estate of salvation by a redeemer.

21. Who is the redeemer of God's elect?

The only redeemer of God's elect is the Lord Jesus Christ, who, being the eternal Son of God, became man, and so was, and continues to be, God and man in two distinct natures, and one person, forever.

22. How did Christ, being the Son of God, become man?

Christ, the Son of God, became man, by taking to himself a true body and a reasonable soul, being conceived by the power of the Holy Ghost, in the womb of the virgin Mary, and born of her, yet without sin.

23. What offices does Christ execute as our redeemer?

Christ, as our redeemer, executes the offices of a prophet, of a priest, and of a king, both in his estate of humiliation and exaltation.

24. How does Christ execute the office of a prophet?

Christ executes the office of a prophet, in revealing to us, by his Word and Spirit, the will of God for our salvation.

25. How does Christ execute the office of a priest?

Christ executes the office of a priest, in his once offering up of himself a sacrifice to satisfy divine justice, and reconcile us to God; and in making continual intercession for us.

26. How does Christ execute the office of a king?

Christ executes the office of a king, in subduing us to himself, in ruling and defending us, and in restraining and conquering all his and our enemies.

27. Wherein did Christ's humiliation consist?

Christ's humiliation consisted in his being born, and that in a low condition, made under the law, undergoing the miseries of this life, the wrath of God, and the cursed death of the cross; in being buried, and continuing under the power of death for a time.

28. Wherein consisted Christ's exaltation?

Christ's exaltation consisted in his rising again from the dead on the third day, in ascending up into heaven, in sitting at the right hand of God the Father, and in coming to judge the world at the last day.

THE BENEFITS OF CHRIST'S WORK

29. How are we made partakers of the redemption purchased by Christ?

We are made partakers of the redemption purchased by Christ, by the effectual application of it to us by his Holy Spirit.

30. How does the Spirit apply to us the redemption purchased by Christ?

The Spirit applies to us the redemption purchased by Christ, by working faith in us, and thereby uniting us to Christ in our effectual calling.

31. What is effectual calling?

Effectual calling is the work of God's Spirit, whereby, convincing us of our sin and misery, enlightening our minds in the knowledge of Christ, and renewing our wills, he does persuade and enable us to embrace Jesus Christ, freely offered to us in the gospel.

32. What benefits do they that are effectually called partake of in this life?

They that are effectually called do in this life partake of justification, adoption, and sanctification, and the several benefits, which in this life, do either accompany or flow from them.

33. What is justification?

Justification is an act of God's free grace, wherein he pardons all our sins, and accepts us as righteous in his sight, only for the righteousness of Christ imputed to us, and received by faith alone.

34. What is adoption?

Adoption is an act of God's free grace, whereby we are received into the number, and have a right to all the privileges of, the sons of God.

35. What is sanctification?

Sanctification is the work of God's free grace, whereby we are renewed in the whole man after the image of God, and are enabled more and more to die unto sin, and live unto righteousness.

36. What are the benefits which in this life do accompany or flow from justification, adoption, and sanctification?

The benefits which in this life do accompany or flow from justification, adoption, and sanctification, are, assurance of God's love, peace of conscience, joy in the Holy Ghost, increase of grace, and perseverance therein to the end.

37. What benefits do believers receive from Christ at death?

The souls of believers are at their death made perfect in holiness, and do immediately pass into glory; and their bodies, being still united to Christ, do rest in their graves till the resurrection.

38. What benefits do believers receive from Christ at the resurrection?

At the resurrection, believers being raised up in glory, shall be openly acknowledged and acquitted in the day of judgment, and made perfectly blessed in the full enjoying of God to all eternity.

THE MORAL LAW:
THE RULE OF OUR OBEDIENCE

39. What is the duty which God requires of man?

The duty which God requires of man is obedience to his revealed will.

40. What did God at first reveal to man for the rule of his obedience?

The rule which God at first revealed to man for his obedience was the moral law.

41. Where is the moral law summarily comprehended?

The moral law is summarily comprehended in the Ten Commandments.

42. What is the sum of the Ten Commandments?

The sum of the Ten Commandments is to love the Lord our God with all our heart, with all our soul, with all our strength, and with all our mind; and our neighbor as ourselves.

PREFACE AND COMMANDMENTS 1-4:
OUR DUTY TO GOD

43. What is the preface to the Ten Commandments?

The preface to the Ten Commandments is in these words, *I am the Lord thy God, which have brought thee out of the land of Egypt, out of the house of bondage.*

44. What does the preface to the Ten Commandments teach us?

The preface to the Ten Commandments teaches us that because God is the Lord, and our God, and redeemer, therefore we are bound to keep all his commandments.

45. Which is the first commandment?

The first commandment is, *Thou shalt have no other gods before me.*

46. What is required in the first commandment?

The first commandment requires us to know and acknowledge God to be the only true God, and our God; and to worship and glorify him accordingly.

47. What is forbidden in the first commandment?

The first commandment forbids the denying, or not worshiping and glorifying the true God as God, and our God; and the giving of that worship and glory to any other, which is due to him alone.

48. What are we specially taught by these words *before me* in the first commandment?

These words *before me* in the first commandment teach us that God, who sees all things, takes notice of, and is much displeased with, the sin of having any other god.

49. Which is the second commandment?

The second commandment is, *Thou shalt not make unto thee any graven image, or any likeness of anything that is in heaven above, or that is in the earth beneath, or that is in the water under the earth: thou shalt not bow down thyself to them, nor serve them: for I the Lord thy God am a jealous God, visiting the iniquity of the fathers upon the children unto the third and fourth generation of them that hate me; and showing mercy unto thousands of them that love me, and keep my commandments.*

50. What is required in the second commandment?

The second commandment requires the receiving, observing, and keeping pure and entire, all such religious worship and ordinances as God has appointed in his Word.

51. What is forbidden in the second commandment?

The second commandment forbids the worshiping of God by images, or any other way not appointed in his Word.

52. What are the reasons annexed to the second commandment?

The reasons annexed to the second commandment are, God's sovereignty over us, his propriety in us, and the zeal he has to his own worship.

53. Which is the third commandment?

The third commandment is, *Thou shalt not take the name of the Lord thy God in vain: for the Lord will not hold him guiltless that taketh his name in vain.*

54. What is required in the third commandment?

The third commandment requires the holy and reverent use of God's names, titles, attributes, ordinances, Word, and works.

55. What is forbidden in the third commandment?

The third commandment forbids all profaning or abusing of anything whereby God makes himself known.

56. What is the reason annexed to the third commandment?

The reason annexed to the third commandment is that however the breakers of this commandment may escape punishment from men, yet the Lord our God will not suffer them to escape his righteous judgment.

57. Which is the fourth commandment?

The fourth commandment is, *Remember the sabbath day, to keep it holy. Six days shalt thou labor, and do all thy work: but the seventh day is the sabbath of the Lord thy God: in it thou shalt not do any work, thou, nor thy son, nor thy daughter, thy manservant, nor thy maidservant, nor thy cattle, nor thy stranger that is within thy gates: for in six days the Lord made heaven and earth, the sea, and all that in them is, and rested the seventh day: wherefore the Lord blessed the sabbath day, and hallowed it.*

58. What is required in the fourth commandment?

The fourth commandment requires the keeping holy to God such set times as he has appointed in his Word; expressly one whole day in seven, to be a holy sabbath to himself.

59. Which day of the seven has God appointed to be the weekly sabbath?

From the beginning of the world to the resurrection of Christ, God appointed the seventh day of the week to be the weekly sabbath; and the first day of the week ever since, to continue to the end of the world, which is the Christian sabbath.

60. How is the sabbath to be sanctified?

The sabbath is to be sanctified by a holy resting all that day, even from such worldly employments and recreations as are lawful on other days; and spending the whole time in the public and private exercises of God's worship, except so much as is to be taken up in the works of necessity and mercy.

61. What is forbidden in the fourth commandment?

The fourth commandment forbids the omission or careless performance of the duties required, and the profaning the day by idleness, or doing that which is in itself sinful, or by unnecessary thoughts, words, or works, about our worldly employments or recreations.

62. What are the reasons annexed to the fourth commandment?

The reasons annexed to the fourth commandment are, God's allowing us six days of the week for our own employments, his challenging a special propriety in the seventh, his own example, and his blessing the sabbath day.

COMMANDMENTS 5-10: OUR DUTY TO MAN

63. Which is the fifth commandment?

The fifth commandment is, *Honor thy father and thy mother; that thy days may be long upon the land which the Lord thy God giveth thee.*

64. What is required in the fifth commandment?

The fifth commandment requires the preserving the honor, and performing the duties, belonging to every one in their several places and relations, as superiors, inferiors, or equals.

65. What is forbidden in the fifth commandment?

The fifth commandment forbids the neglecting of, or doing anything against, the honor and duty which belong to every one in their several places and relations.

66. What is the reason annexed to the fifth commandment?

The reason annexed to the fifth commandment is a promise of long life and prosperity (as far as it shall serve for God's glory and their own good) to all such as keep this commandment.

67. Which is the sixth commandment?

The sixth commandment is, *Thou shalt not kill.*

68. What is required in the sixth commandment?

The sixth commandment requires all lawful endeavors to preserve our own life, and the life of others.

69. What is forbidden in the sixth commandment?

The sixth commandment forbids the taking away of our own life, or the life of our neighbor unjustly, or whatsoever tends thereunto.

70. Which is the seventh commandment?

The seventh commandment is, *Thou shalt not commit adultery.*

71. What is required in the seventh commandment?

The seventh commandment requires the preservation of our own and our neighbor's chastity, in heart, speech, and behavior.

72. What is forbidden in the seventh commandment?

The seventh commandment forbids all unchaste thoughts, words, and actions.

73. Which is the eighth commandment?

The eighth commandment is, *Thou shalt not steal.*

74. What is required in the eighth commandment?

The eighth commandment requires the lawful procuring and furthering the wealth and outward estate of ourselves and others.

75. What is forbidden in the eighth commandment?

The eighth commandment forbids whatsoever does or may unjustly hinder our own or our neighbor's wealth or outward estate.

76. Which is the ninth commandment?

The ninth commandment is, *Thou shalt not bear false witness against thy neighbor.*

77. What is required in the ninth commandment?

The ninth commandment requires the maintaining and promoting of truth between man and man, and of our own and our neighbor's good name, especially in witness-bearing.

78. What is forbidden in the ninth commandment?

The ninth commandment forbids whatsoever is prejudicial to truth, or injurious to our own or our neighbor's good name.

79. Which is the tenth commandment?

The tenth commandment is, *Thou shalt not covet thy neighbor's house, thou shalt not covet thy neighbor's wife, nor his manservant, nor his maidservant, nor his ox, nor his ass, nor anything that is thy neighbor's.*

80. What is required in the tenth commandment?

The tenth commandment requires full contentment with our own condition, with a right and charitable frame of spirit toward our neighbor, and all that is his.

81. What is forbidden in the tenth commandment?

The tenth commandment forbids all discontentment with our own estate, envying or grieving at the good of our neighbor, and all inordinate motions and affections to anything that is his.

OUR FALLEN CONDITION AND
THE CONSEQUENCE OF SIN

82. Is any man able perfectly to keep the commandments of God?

No mere man since the fall is able in this life perfectly to keep the commandments of God, but does daily break them in thought, word, and deed

83. Are all transgressions of the law equally heinous?

Some sins in themselves, and by reason of several aggravations, are more heinous in the sight of God than others.

84. What does every sin deserve?

Every sin deserves God's wrath and curse, both in this life, and that which is to come.

FAITH, REPENTANCE, AND
THE ORDINARY MEANS OF SALVATION

85. What does God require of us that we may escape his wrath and curse due to us for sin?

To escape the wrath and curse of God due to us for sin, God requires of us faith in Jesus Christ, repentance unto life, with the diligent use of all the outward means whereby Christ communicates to us the benefits of redemption.

86. What is faith in Jesus Christ?

Faith in Jesus Christ is a saving grace, whereby we receive and rest upon him alone for salvation, as he is offered to us in the gospel.

87. What is repentance unto life?

Repentance unto life is a saving grace, whereby a sinner, out of a true sense of his sin, and apprehension of the mercy of God in Christ, does, with grief and hatred of his sin, turn from it unto God, with full purpose of, and endeavor after, new obedience.

88. What are the outward and ordinary means whereby Christ communicates to us the benefits of redemption?

The outward and ordinary means whereby Christ communicates to us the benefits of redemption, are his ordinances, especially the Word, sacraments, and prayer; all which are made effectual to the elect for salvation.

ORDINARY MEANS OF SALVATION: THE WORD OF GOD

89. How is the Word made effectual to salvation?

The Spirit of God makes the reading, but especially the preaching, of the Word, an effectual means of convincing and converting sinners, and of building them up in holiness and comfort, through faith, unto salvation.

90. How is the Word to be read and heard, that it may become effectual to salvation?

That the Word may become effectual to salvation, we must attend thereunto with diligence, preparation, and prayer; receive it with faith and love, lay it up in our hearts, and practice it in our lives.

ORDINARY MEANS OF SALVATION: THE SACRAMENTS

91. How do the sacraments become effectual means of salvation?

The sacraments become effectual means of salvation, not from any virtue in them, or in him that does administer them; but only by the blessing of Christ, and the working of his Spirit in them that by faith receive them.

92. What is a sacrament?

A sacrament is a holy ordinance instituted by Christ; wherein, by sensible signs, Christ, and the benefits of the new covenant, are represented, sealed, and applied to believers.

93. Which are the sacraments of the New Testament?

The sacraments of the New Testament are baptism and the Lord's Supper.

94. What is baptism?

Baptism is a sacrament, wherein the washing with water in the name of the Father, and of the Son, and of the Holy Ghost, does signify and seal our ingrafting into Christ, and partaking of the benefits of the covenant of grace, and our engagement to be the Lord's.

95. To whom is baptism to be administered?

Baptism is not to be administered to any that are out of the visible church, till they profess their faith in Christ, and obedience to him; but the infants of such as are members of the visible church are to be baptized.

96. What is the Lord's Supper?

The Lord's Supper is a sacrament, wherein, by giving and receiving bread and wine according to Christ's appointment, his death is showed forth; and the worthy receivers are, not after a corporal and carnal manner, but by faith, made partakers of his body and blood, with all his benefits, to their spiritual nourishment and growth in grace.

97. What is required to the worthy receiving of the Lord's Supper?

It is required of them that would worthily partake of the Lord's Supper, that they examine themselves of their knowledge to discern the Lord's body, of their faith to feed upon him, of their repentance, love, and new obedience; lest, coming unworthily, they eat and drink judgment to themselves.

ORDINARY MEANS OF SALVATION: PRAYER

98. What is prayer?

Prayer is an offering up of our desires unto God, for things agreeable to his will, in the name of Christ, with confession of our sins, and thankful acknowledgment of his mercies.

99. What rule has God given for our direction in prayer?

The whole Word of God is of use to direct us in prayer; but the special rule of direction is that form of prayer which Christ taught his disciples, commonly called the Lord's Prayer.

100. What does the preface of the Lord's Prayer teach us?

The preface of the Lord's prayer, which is, *Our Father which art in heaven*, teaches us to draw near to God with all holy reverence and confidence, as children to a father able and ready to help us; and that we should pray with and for others.

101. What do we pray for in the first petition?

In the first petition, which is, *Hallowed be thy name*, we pray that God would enable us and others to glorify him in all that whereby he makes himself known; and that he would dispose all things to his own glory.

102. What do we pray for in the second petition?

In the second petition, which is, *Thy kingdom come*, we pray that Satan's kingdom may be destroyed; and that the kingdom of grace may be advanced, ourselves and others brought into it, and kept in it; and that the kingdom of glory may be hastened.

103. What do we pray for in the third petition?

In the third petition, which is, *Thy will be done in earth, as it is in heaven*, we pray that God, by his grace, would make us able and willing to know, obey, and submit to his will in all things, as the angels do in heaven.

104. What do we pray for in the fourth petition?

In the fourth petition, which is, *Give us this day our daily bread*, we pray that of God's free gift we may receive a competent portion of the good things of this life, and enjoy his blessing with them.

105. What do we pray for in the fifth petition?

In the fifth petition, which is, *And forgive us our debts, as we forgive our debtors*, we pray that God, for Christ's sake, would freely pardon all our sins; which we are the rather encouraged to ask, because by his grace we are enabled from the heart to forgive others.

106. What do we pray for in the sixth petition?

In the sixth petition, which is, *And lead us not into temptation, but deliver us from evil,* we pray that God would either keep us from being tempted to sin, or support and deliver us when we are tempted.

107. What does the conclusion of the Lord's Prayer teach us?

The conclusion of the Lord's Prayer, which is, *For thine is the kingdom, and the power, and the glory, forever, Amen,* teaches us to take our encouragement in prayer from God only, and in our prayers to praise him, ascribing kingdom, power, and glory to him. And in testimony of our desire, and assurance to be heard, we say, Amen.

Grammar Catechisms
By Grade Level

PHILOSOPHICAL FOUNDATION GRAMMAR

General Revelation

KINDERGARTEN

1. What is epistemology?

Epistemology answers the question: how do we know?

2. How do we have knowledge?

We know by reason and argument.

3. What is reason in itself?

Reason in itself is the laws of thought.

4. What are the three laws of thought?

The laws of thought are: the law of identity, the law of non-contradiction, and the law of excluded middle.

5. What is reason in its use?

Reason in its use is formative, critical, interpretive, and constructive.

6. What are the three forms of thought resulting from the three acts of reason?

We use reason to form concepts, judgments, and arguments.

7. What is a concept?

In a concept, the mind grasps the essential nature of a being, class of beings, or aspect of beings.

8. What is an essence?

An essence is the set of qualities that all members of a class and only members always have, and distinguishes them from all non-members.

9. How is a concept expressed?

A concept is expressed by a term; a term is a word or group of words.

10. What is a judgment?

In a judgment, the mind relates two concepts by affirmation or negation.

11. How is a judgment expressed?

A judgment is expressed in a statement.

FIRST GRADE

12. What is an argument?

In an argument, premises are given as reasons to support a conclusion.

13. What is a valid argument?

An argument is valid if the premises logically support the conclusion.

14. What is a sound argument?

An argument is sound if it is valid and its premises are true.

15. How is reason used critically?

Reason is used critically as a test for meaning.

16. How is reason used to interpret?

Reason is used to interpret (or give meaning to) experience in light of one's basic beliefs.

17. How is reason used constructively?

Reason is used to construct a coherent world and life view.

18. What is reason in us?

Reason in us is natural, ontological, transcendental, and fundamental.

19. How is reason natural?

Reason is universal; it is the same in all persons at all times.

20. How is reason ontological?

Reason applies to being as well as thought.

21. How is reason transcendental?

Reason is self-attesting and the highest authority.

22. How is reason fundamental?

Reason is basic to other aspects of human personality.

23. What is our presupposition?

Our presupposition is our set of basic beliefs used to give meaning to our experience.

24. What are the three areas and questions in each set of basic beliefs?

Epistemology—how do we know?; Metaphysics—what is real?; Ethics—what ought I to do?

25. What is the basic pair of beliefs in epistemology?

The basic pair of beliefs in epistemology is: knowledge is possible, that is, some things are clear vs. knowledge is not possible and basic things are not clear.

26. What is the basic pair of beliefs in metaphysics?

The basic pair of beliefs in metaphysics is: only some is eternal (God) vs. all is eternal (in some form or other).

27. What is the basic pair of beliefs in ethics?

The basic pair of beliefs in ethics is: the good is the end in itself vs. the good is virtue or happiness.

28. Who holds to which of the basic beliefs?

We are more or less conscious and consistent in our basic beliefs; each person holds an admixture of both; there is a conflict of unbelief in the believer and belief in the unbeliever.

29. What should be our response to this conflict?

Our response should be to be more conscious and consistent in our basic beliefs.

30. How does history relate to this conflict?

History is an outworking of this conflict in each person and between all persons.

31. What will be the outcome of this conflict?

Only what retains meaning can last; meaning will overcome meaninglessness; light will overcome darkness; good will overcome evil.

SECOND GRADE

32. What is metaphysics?

Metaphysics answers the question: what is real or eternal?

33. What is our most basic concept?

Our most basic concept is eternal existence.

34. What is meant by eternal?

Eternal means what has always existed and will always exist.

35. What are the most basic answers to the question: what is eternal?

Either all is eternal, or none is eternal, or only some is eternal.

36. What kinds of things exist?

What exists is either matter or spirit.

37. What are the essential qualities of matter?

Matter in itself is non-living; it has size in space, but no consciousness.

38. What are the essential qualities of spirit?

Spirit has no size, but it is conscious.

39. Who believes all is eternal?

Material monists, spiritual monists, and dualists believe all is eternal.

40. What is material monism?

Material monism is the belief that all is matter and matter is eternal.

41. What is spiritual monism?

Spiritual monism is the belief that all is spirit and spirit is eternal.

42. What is dualism?

Dualism is the belief that both matter and spirit exist and both matter and spirit are eternal.

43. Who believes only some is eternal?

Theists and deists believe only God is eternal.

44. What is the difference between theists and deists?

Theists believe God created and rules; deists believe God created but does not rule.

45. Who believes none is eternal?

Buddhism teaches that all is *dukkha*, that only change or process is real.

46. Must there be something eternal?

If nothing is eternal, then being must have come into existence from non-being, which is impossible.

47. Is matter eternal?

If matter were eternal, it would be self-maintaining, but matter is not self-maintaining.

48. Is everything made of matter?

The mind is not the brain; matter cannot explain human thinking or seeing.

49. Is the soul eternal?

If the soul (or mind) were eternal, it would know everything, but we do not know everything, so the soul is not eternal.

50. Does the material world exist?

The cause of what I see is not my mind or another mind, but outside all minds.

51. Can there be only one mind and its ideas?

The world cannot be an illusion (*maya*) in the one mind which knows everything.

52. Are we all part of one mind (God)?

We cannot be infinite and eternal or finite and eternal.

THIRD GRADE

53. Why did God create?

God created because he is, and he reveals his glory by creation.

54. Who made God?

There must be something eternal, and only God is eternal.

55. What is God?

God is a spirit who is infinite, eternal, and unchangeable, in his power and wisdom.

56. Is God good?

God created man with a concern for goodness; therefore, God is good.

57. What is moral evil?

Moral evil is an act contrary to one's nature as a rational being; it is to neglect, avoid, resist, and deny (NARD) reason.

58. What is natural evil?

Natural evil is suffering due to external circumstance; it is toil and strife, and old age, sickness, and death.

59. Did God create the world good?

Because God is all good and all-powerful, he could, would, must, and did create the world without any evil.

60. Why is there moral evil?

Moral evil serves to deepen the revelation of God's glory.

61. What is the inherent consequence of moral evil?

The inherent consequence of moral evil is meaninglessness, boredom, and guilt.

62. Why is there natural evil?

Natural evil is imposed by God to restrain, recall from, and remove moral evil; it is a call to stop and think.

63. Will natural evil be removed?

Natural evil will be removed when moral evil is removed.

64. Will moral evil be removed?

Moral evil is gradually removed as unbelief in every form is overcome by belief.

65. How can God be both just and merciful to man in moral evil?

Special revelation is required to know how God can be both just and merciful.

66. Does special revelation exist?

Special revelation exists if it is consistent with clear general revelation and shows how God is both just and merciful.

67. What is ethics?

Ethics answers the question: what is the good?

68. At the most basic level, what is the good?

The good is the end in itself; it is sought for its own sake; it is the highest value.

69. What is virtue?

Virtue is a means to the good; virtue is not the good.

70. What are the three kinds of virtue?

The three kinds of virtue are moral, natural, and instrumental.

71. What is happiness?

Happiness is the effect of possessing what one believes is the good; happiness is not the good.

72. What is lasting happiness?

Lasting happiness is the effect of possessing what is truly the good.

73. What is the means to the good?

The means to the good is the moral law through the work of dominion.

74. What is the good for a being?

The good for a being is according to the nature of that being.

75. What is the good for man?

The good for man as a rational being is the use of reason to the fullest; reason is used to understand the nature of things; the nature of things created reveals the nature of God; the good for man is the knowledge of God.

76. What are the 10 formal characteristics of the good?

The good is continuing, inexhaustible, comprehensive, inalienable, corporate, cumulative, communal, fulfilling, ultimate, and transformative.

77. How is the good the source of unity?

The good is given in human nature, which is one and the same for all; therefore, it is the source of unity in each person and among all persons.

78. What are the three most basic characteristics of the moral law?

The moral law is clear, comprehensive, and critical.

79. How is the moral law clear?

The moral law is given in human nature, which is easily knowable by all human beings.

80. How is the moral law comprehensive?

The moral law guides all choices that express all aspects of human nature.

81. How is the moral law critical?

The moral law has inherent consequences of spiritual life or death.

FOURTH GRADE

82. What is moral law 1 about?

Moral law 1 is about the good and the real.

83. How is moral law 1 given in human nature?

By nature, we make choices concerning means and ends; the end in itself is the good, which is grounded in what is eternal.

84. What is moral law 2 about?

Moral law 2 is about the nature of thinking and the divine nature.

85. How is moral law 2 given in human nature?

By nature, we think, and thinking by nature is presuppositional; we must think of the finite (man) in light of the infinite (God).

86. What is moral law 3 about?

Moral law 3 is about unity and integrity.

87. How is moral law 3 given in human nature?

Human nature is one, which is a natural unity; to be undivided we must be concerned for consistency.

88. What is moral law 4 about?

Moral law 4 is about work and rest.

89. How is moral law 4 given in human nature?

By nature, the work of dominion is necessary to achieve the good; when the good is achieved, work will cease.

90. What is moral law 5 about?

Moral law 5 is about authority and insight.

91. How is moral law 5 given in human nature?

By nature, we are born ignorant, and by nature, we need teaching based on insight into the good and the means to the good.

92. What is moral law 6 about?

Moral law 6 is about human dignity and rationality.

93. How is moral law 6 given in human nature?

We are born human, with a capacity to understand that distinguishes man from animal.

94. What is moral law 7 about?

Moral law 7 is about spiritual fidelity and infidelity.

95. How is moral law 7 given in human nature?

We are born of a sexual union between one man and one woman; ordinary fidelity is based on fidelity to the good.

96. What is moral law 8 about?

Moral law 8 is about talent and value.

97. How is moral law 8 given in human nature?

We are each born with some talent; by talent, we achieve some aspect of the good.

98. What is moral law 9 about?

Moral law 9 is about truth and justice.

99. How is moral law 9 given in human nature?

We are born equal and, in justice, equals are treated equally; truth is necessary and sufficient for justice.

100. What is moral law 10 about?

Moral law 10 is about contentment and the good.

101. How is moral law 10 given in human nature?

We are born changeable in our understanding; discontent arises from a misunderstanding of good and evil.

102. What is the work of dominion?

The work of dominion is given to man, made in the image of God, and consists in naming and ruling the creation.

103. How does man name and rule in the natural world and in the human world?

Man names and rules in the natural world by science and technology, and in the human world by the humanities and the arts.

104. Given moral and natural evil in the world, how can the work of dominion be accomplished?

Under creation–fall–redemption, Christ in the place of Adam will undo what Adam did, and will do what Adam failed to do by subduing all things to himself.

105. How does Christ subdue all things to himself?

Christ subdues all things by making disciples of all nations, teaching them to observe all he commands, and so brings mankind from the Garden of Eden to the City of God.

106. What is the two-fold outcome of the completed work of Christ?

The outcome of Christ's work is that every thought raised up against the knowledge of God will be taken captive, and the earth will be full of the knowledge of the Lord as the waters cover the sea.

THEOLOGICAL FOUNDATION GRAMMAR

Special Revelation: Genesis 1–3

KINDERGARTEN

13. What is the first point of Creation?
Creation is revelation: necessarily, intentionally, and exclusively.

25. What is the second point of Creation?
The revelation is full and clear.

35. What is the third point of Creation?
Eternal life is knowing God (John 17:3).

40. What is the fourth point of Creation?
The knowledge of God is through the work of dominion.

47. What is the fifth point of Creation?
The earth shall be full of the knowledge of the Lord as the waters cover the sea (Isaiah 11:9).

52. What is the first point of the Fall?
The covenant of creation: representation, probation, and manifestation; the covenant of marriage.

63. What is the second point of the Fall?

Temptation: the purpose, the agent, and the argument.

72. What is the third point of the Fall?

Sin: not seeking, not understanding, and not doing what is right.

77. What is the fourth point of the Fall?

Death: two kinds of death: physical and spiritual; the wages of sin is spiritual death.

82. What is the fifth point of the Fall?

Theodicy: why is there evil? Evil deepens the divine revelation.

87. What is the first point of Redemption?

The first call back to repentance: shame (inward/conscience). The first response: self-deception (cover up).

92. What is the second point of Redemption?

The second call back: self-examination (outward/the question: where are you?). The second response: self-justification (blaming others).

98. What is the third point of Redemption?

The third call back: the promise and the curse. The third response: repentance and faith (Adam names his wife Eve).

108. What is the fourth point of Redemption?

Justification: forgiveness of sin through the death of another (the coats of skin).

111. What is the fifth point of Redemption?

Sanctification: cleansing from sin through suffering (the expulsion).

FIRST GRADE

13. What is the first point of Creation?

Creation is revelation: necessarily, intentionally, and exclusively.

14. What general principle is to be understood from *creation is revelation*?

The visible reveals the invisible; the physical reveals the spiritual; the creation reveals the Creator.

15. How is creation revelation necessarily?

The act of a being reveals the nature of that being; the acts of God in creation and providence reveal the nature of God.

16. How is creation revelation intentionally?

Creation was very good; it was what God intended; God intends to be known through his acts.

17. How is creation revelation exclusively?

There is no revelation of God apart from his works of creation and providence.

18. What are the two types of creation?

The two types of creation are original and subsequent creation.

19. What is original creation?

Original creation is *ex nihilo*.

20. What is meant by creation *ex nihilo*?

God brought the substance of creation into being out of nothing; there was no pre-existent material.

21. What does creation *ex nihilo* reveal about God?

Creation *ex nihilo* reveals that only God the Creator is infinite, eternal, and unchangeable.

22. When did time begin?

Time began with the beginning of creation.

23. What new work of God begins upon creation *ex nihilo*?

Upon creation, God begins his work of providence: the Spirit of God moves upon the face of the waters.

24. What is subsequent creation?

Subsequent creation is God forming and filling the cosmos after original creation.

25. What is the second point of Creation?

The revelation is full and clear.

26. In general, how is the revelation full?

The whole earth is full of his glory (Isaiah 6:3); everything in creation and providence reveals God's glory.

27. What is special creation?

Special creation is God directly creating each kind of living creature.

28. Specifically, how is the revelation full?

The vast array of the creation, each after its kind, and the multitudes of human beings in history are a full revelation of God's glory.

29. How are we given a full revelation of God's justice and mercy?

A full revelation of God's justice and mercy is given in providence of the Fall and of redemption.

30. How is the revelation clear?

God's eternal power and divine nature are clearly revealed in the things that are made (Romans 1:20); the law of God is written on the hearts of all men (Romans 2:14-15).

31. Are all men responsible to know this clear revelation?

The clarity of general revelation makes the unbelief of mankind without excuse.

32. How was man created?

Man was created in the image of God, male and female.

33. What is meant by man is the image of God?

Man is finite, temporal, and changeable in his being, wisdom, power, holiness, justice, goodness, and truth.

34. What are male and female?

Male and female are both aspects of the image of God; they are spiritual characteristics in God, and come from God.

SECOND GRADE

1. What are the seven senses of the Word of God?

The Word of God (the Logos) 1) is eternal—the Son of God, 2) is in all men as reason, 3) is in creation as clear general revelation, 4) is in history as special revelation (Scripture), 5) is incarnate in Jesus Christ, 6) is in the Church, by the Holy Spirit, as the Historic Christian Faith, and 7) is in each believer by regeneration and sanctification.

2. What is general revelation?

General revelation is what can be known of God from the creation; it can be known by all men, everywhere, at all times.

3. What is special revelation?

Special revelation is what can be known of God from Scripture; Scripture is given by God for the redemption of man.

4. What does Scripture as redemptive revelation assume?

Scripture assumes the reality of sin in the rejection of the Word of God in man as reason and in the creation as clear general revelation.

5. Why is Scripture necessary?

Scripture is necessary to show how God is both just and merciful to man in sin.

6. How does Scripture show God is both just and merciful to man in sin?

Scripture focuses on the person and work of Christ, the Word of God incarnate, who restores mankind to life in the knowledge of God.

7. What is assumed in reading and understanding Scripture?

The use of reason and knowledge of clear general revelation are assumed in reading and understanding Scripture.

8. What is meant in saying Scripture is organic?

Scripture is a unity that grows; from the beginning, the foundation of Scripture is given in organic seed form.

9. What is Foundation (Philosophical, Theological, and Historical) necessary for?

Foundation is necessary to go on to maturity, fruitfulness, unity of the faith, and fullness of the knowledge of God (Ephesians 4; Hebrews 6).

10. Where is Theological Foundation given in Scripture?

Theological Foundation is given in Genesis 1–3.

11. What is meant in saying Genesis 1–3 is Theological Foundation?

Scripture builds on, is to be understood by, and is the development of what is revealed in Genesis 1–3; understanding the beginning is necessary for understanding all that follows.

12. What are the three basic themes of Theological Foundation?

The three basic themes of Theological Foundation are: Creation, Fall, and Redemption.

35. What is the third point of Creation?

Eternal life is knowing God (John 17:3).

36. What is meant by eternal life?

Our knowledge of God begins in this life and grows unendingly in the next life.

37. How is eternal life referred to in general revelation (Philosophical Foundation)?

From general revelation, the good is the knowledge of God.

38. How is eternal life referred to in Historic Christianity (Historical Foundation)?

From Historic Christianity, man's chief end is to glorify God and to enjoy him forever.

39. What does it mean to glorify God?

To glorify God is to know his glory and to make his glory known.

40. What is the fourth point of Creation?

The knowledge of God is through the work of dominion.

41. How did God bless man in relation to the work of dominion?

God blessed man to be fruitful and multiply, to fill the earth and subdue it and to rule over it.

42. What two aspects are included in the call to dominion?

In dominion, man is called to name the creation and to rule over it.

43. How does man name the creation?

Man names the creation in grasping the nature of all beings in all their parts and relations.

44. When does naming the creation begin and end?

God begins naming in his work of creation, and man as the image of God continues until everything is named.

45. How does man rule over the creation?

Man rules over the creation by developing the powers latent in himself and in the creation so as to make known the glory of God.

46. How is the work of dominion to be achieved?

The work of dominion is to be achieved by all of mankind working together through all of history.

47. What is the fifth point of Creation?

The earth shall be full of the knowledge of the Lord as the waters cover the sea (Isaiah 11:9).

48. How does God signify that his work of creation is complete?

God signifies that his work of creation is complete by blessing the seventh day and calling it holy—the Sabbath day.

49. What does the Sabbath signify for man as the image of God?

As God completed the work of creation, so man will complete the work of dominion.

50. Why is the Sabbath to be observed by all men?

The Sabbath is a perpetual reminder to man of his origin, destiny, and hope.

51. What was the condition of original creation?

Original creation was very good; there was no moral or natural evil; animals were given the green vegetation for food, and humans did not die.

THIRD GRADE

52. What is the first point of the Fall?

The covenant of creation: representation, probation, and manifestation; the covenant of marriage.

53. Where is the covenant of creation given in Scripture?

The covenant of creation is given in Genesis 2.

54. What is the purpose of the covenant of creation?

It is the purpose of the LORD God to establish mankind in a permanent relationship with himself.

55. What is meant by mankind being established in a permanent relationship with the LORD?

The LORD's gracious purpose is to bring man from a state in which he could fall away in sin, to a state in which he is established in righteousness.

56. How is the doctrine of covenant representation revealed in general?

The Garden of Eden is the biological, geographical, and historical center of life on earth; all life flows out from this center.

57. What is visibly represented by the two trees at the center of all life in Eden?

All of life is centered in man's choice between two ways: good and evil, life and death.

58. How is the doctrine of covenant representation revealed particularly?

As covenant head of the human race, Adam represents the entire human race; the act of one man will affect all.

59. What is meant by probation in the covenant of creation?

Adam is to be tested concerning his pursuit of God's purpose for mankind: the knowledge of God through the work of dominion.

60. What is meant by manifestation in the covenant of creation?

The inward, invisible choice of good and evil is manifested in the outward act of obedience regarding eating from the two trees.

61. What does the visible covenant of marriage reveal?

The visible covenant of marriage between man and woman reveals the invisible covenant of creation between God and man.

62. In what moral state was man created?

Man was created in a state of moral innocence and purity; they felt no shame in either their inward or outward condition.

63. What is the second point of the Fall?

Temptation: the purpose, the agent, and the argument.

64. What is the purpose of the temptation?

The temptation is a test of one's faith or understanding of good and evil; it serves to reveal the inward condition of man, whether he has been seeking the knowledge of God as the good.

65. What purpose does the agent of temptation serve?

Neither the agent nor the temptation is the cause of sin, but rather the outward occasion that reveals sin.

66. In what form does the test of temptation come?

The temptation comes in the form of an argument addressed to the understanding.

67. What two parts of the argument can be identified?

A reason or premise ("for you shall be like God knowing good and evil") is given to support the conclusion ("you shall not surely die").

68. In saying, "you shall not surely die," what is the tempter denying?

The tempter, who is the devil, denies the Word of God regarding the inherent consequence of spiritual death for disobeying God's command.

69. In saying, "for you shall be like God knowing good and evil," what is the tempter offering?

The tempter offers the impossible promise of man becoming like God in how he knows good and evil.

70. Why is the promise of man becoming like God in knowing good and evil impossible?

God as the infinite Creator knows good and evil by determining it in the act of creating; man as a finite creature knows good and evil by discovering it according to God's creation.

71. What inward reality is revealed in the outward act of eating from the tree of the knowledge of good and evil?

Man had ceased seeking to know God and so failed to understand the clear difference between God the Creator and man the creature with respect to knowing good and evil; instead, man had put himself in the place of God to determine good and evil.

72. What is the third point of the Fall?

Sin: not seeking, not understanding, and not doing what is right.

73. What was the immediate cause of man's disobedience in eating the forbidden fruit?

Man put the desire for beauty, pleasure, and wisdom apart from God above the love of God.

74. What does the account of the Fall of man particularly reveal?

The account of the Fall of man particularly reveals original sin.

75. What is meant by original sin?

Original sin is the first sin in the history of mankind, and it is how sin at its root originates in all.

76. What is meant by root sin and fruit sin?

The root sin of not seeking and not understanding leads to the fruit sin of not doing what is right.

77. What is the fourth point of the Fall?

Death: two kinds of death: physical and spiritual; the wages of sin is spiritual death.

78. In general, what is spiritual death?

Spiritual death is the inherent consequence of sin; it is present and inherent in sin, not future and imposed.

79. Inwardly, what is spiritual death?

Inwardly, spiritual death is meaninglessness, boredom, and guilt, increasing without end.

80. Outwardly, what is spiritual death?

Outwardly, spiritual death is the breakdown and reversal of the order established by creation.

81. How does physical death reveal spiritual death?

Physical death is imposed by God as a call back from spiritual death.

82. What is the fifth point of the Fall?

Theodicy: why is there evil? Evil deepens the divine revelation.

83. How does evil deepen the divine revelation?

The revelation of the divine justice and mercy particularly is deepened.

84. How is the divine justice deepened in permitting evil?

Justice is revealed in the connection between sin and death; moral evil as unbelief is allowed to work itself out in world history in every form and degree of admixture with belief.

85. How is the divine mercy deepened in imposing natural evil?

Mercy is revealed in redemption; natural evil is imposed by God to restrain, recall from, and remove moral evil; as a call back, natural evil requires redemptive revelation to show how God is both just and merciful, at the same time, to man in sin.

86. How is moral evil being removed?

Moral evil is removed gradually; if it is removed abruptly, then the revelation will not be deepened; if it is not removed, then the revelation will not be seen.

FOURTH GRADE

87. What is the first point of Redemption?

The first call back to repentance: shame (inward/conscience). The first response: self-deception (cover up).

88. What was the immediate effect of the loss of righteousness through disobedience?

The immediate effect of the loss of righteousness through disobedience was that they realized their spiritual nakedness, now manifest in their visible nakedness, and felt ashamed.

89. How does the visible reveal the invisible in the state of sin?

Under sin, physical nakedness is a reminder of spiritual nakedness.

90. What was the outward response to the shame of nakedness?

Shame is avoided by making a covering of leaves, yet the covering is still seen and still reminds.

91. What was the inward response to the shame of nakedness?

By self-deception, one avoids acknowledging the sin of not seeking and not understanding what is clear about God.

92. What is the second point of Redemption?

The second call back: self-examination (outward/the question: where are you?). The second response: self-justification (blaming others).

93. How does the second call back go beyond the first call back?

The second call back is outer and from another (God) vs. inward and from within oneself.

94. In asking, "Where are you?" what is God calling for?

In asking, "Where are you?" God, who is all-knowing, is calling man to examine himself.

95. In asking, "Have you eaten from the tree of which I commanded you . . .?" what is God calling for?

In asking, "Have you eaten from the tree of which I commanded you…?" God is calling man who is hiding in guilt and fear to confess his sin.

96. How does man seek to justify himself in response to the second call back?

Man seeks to justify himself by blaming others, both the woman and God, for his own act of disobedience.

97. Instead of seeking to justify himself, what should man have seen?

Man, in sin, cannot justify himself before God; he must rely only on God's mercy.

98. What is the third point of Redemption?

The third call back: the promise and the curse. The third response: repentance and faith (Adam names his wife Eve).

99. How does the third call back go beyond the second call back?

The third call back is given in deed, beyond word; it is the final and lasting call back.

100. What is the promise?

The promise is that through a spiritual war, which is age-long and agonizing, good will overcome evil.

101. What will the seed of the woman (the Second Adam—Christ) do in place of the first Adam?

The seed of the woman will undo what Adam did (by paying the penalty for sin) and do what Adam failed to do (by filling the earth with the knowledge of God through the work of dominion).

102. What is the curse?

The curse consists of toil and strife, and old age, sickness, and death.

103. At times, how is the curse intensified corporately?

The curse is intensified corporately to war, famine, and plague.

104. Why is the curse to be understood as the mercy of God and not punishment (justice)?

The curse is merciful in that it is imposed by God as the final, continuing call back from sin and self-deception and self-justification; the curse is not punishment, which is inherent in sin.

105. How is the curse to be understood in relation to covenant representation?

The curse is imposed by God on all mankind as a call back from sin through Adam's representation.

106. When will the curse (or natural evil) be removed?

The curse will be removed when sin (or moral evil) is removed and there is no more natural evil as a call to repentance.

107. What response is given by man to the promise and curse?

Man chooses to obey in repentance by accepting life for mankind under the curse, with faith and hope in the promise of redemption.

108. What is the fourth point of Redemption?

Justification: forgiveness of sin through the death of another (the coats of skin).

109. What is God's first response to man's faith in his promise?

God justifies man by covering his guilt through vicarious atonement—through the sacrifice of another in the place of Adam; man is given the garment of skin to cover his nakedness.

110. Under covenant representation, what is triple imputation?

Adam's guilt is imputed to all whom he represents; the guilt of all who accept the promise is imputed to the one promised in the place of Adam; the righteousness of the one sacrificed is imputed to all who believe.

111. What is the fifth point of Redemption?

Sanctification: cleansing from sin through suffering (the expulsion).

112. What is God's second response to man's faith?

God expels man from the Garden, to live under the effects of the curse, to be sanctified (cleansed) from sin and self-deception and self-justification.

113. By what means is man sanctified?

Sanctification is by knowledge of the truth; this knowledge comes through suffering under the curse.

114. Why can the call back through the curse not be avoided?

There is no life apart from the knowledge of God, and under sin, there is no knowledge of God apart from suffering in the work of dominion; the way to the tree of life is guarded, and all born of Adam must die physically.

115. For those who are justified, when is sanctification complete?

Sanctification for those who are justified continues until death; it is incomplete until death and ends with death.

HISTORICAL FOUNDATION

GRAMMAR

Historic Christianity:
The Westminster Shorter Catechism

KINDERGARTEN

1. What is the chief end of man?

Man's chief end is to glorify God, and to enjoy him forever.

2. What rule has God given to direct us how we may glorify and enjoy him?

The Word of God, which is contained in the Scriptures of the Old and New Testaments, is the only rule to direct us how we may glorify and enjoy him.

3. What do the Scriptures principally teach?

The Scriptures principally teach what man is to believe concerning God, and what duty God requires of man.

4. What is God?

God is a spirit, infinite, eternal, and unchangeable, in his being, wisdom, power, holiness, justice, goodness, and truth.

5. Are there more Gods than one?

There is but one only, the living and true God.

6. How many persons are there in the Godhead?

There are three persons in the Godhead; the Father, the Son, and the Holy Ghost; and these three are one God, the same in substance, equal in power and glory.

7. What are the decrees of God?

The decrees of God are his eternal purpose, according to the counsel of his will, whereby, for his own glory, he has foreordained whatsoever comes to pass.

8. How does God execute his decrees?

God executes his decrees in the works of creation and providence.

FIRST GRADE

The Ten Commandments

45. Which is the first commandment?

The first commandment is, *Thou shalt have no other gods before me.*

49. Which is the second commandment?

The second commandment is, *Thou shalt not make unto thee any graven image, or any likeness of anything that is in heaven above, or that is in the earth beneath, or that is in the water under the earth: thou shalt not bow down thyself to them, nor serve them: for I the Lord thy God am a jealous God, visiting the iniquity of the fathers upon the children unto the third and fourth generation of them that hate me; and showing mercy unto thousands of them that love me, and keep my commandments.*

53. Which is the third commandment?

The third commandment is, *Thou shalt not take the name of the Lord thy God in vain: for the Lord will not hold him guiltless that taketh his name in vain.*

57. Which is the fourth commandment?

The fourth commandment is, *Remember the sabbath day, to keep it holy. Six days shalt thou labor, and do all thy work: but the seventh day is the sabbath of the Lord thy God: in it thou shalt not do any work, thou, nor thy son, nor thy daughter, thy manservant, nor thy maidservant, nor thy cattle, nor thy stranger that is within thy gates: for in six days the Lord made heaven and earth, the sea, and all that in them is, and rested the seventh day: wherefore the Lord blessed the sabbath day, and hallowed it.*

63. Which is the fifth commandment?

The fifth commandment is, *Honor thy father and thy mother; that thy days may be long upon the land which the Lord thy God giveth thee.*

67. Which is the sixth commandment?

The sixth commandment is, *Thou shalt not kill.*

70. Which is the seventh commandment?

The seventh commandment is, *Thou shalt not commit adultery.*

73. Which is the eighth commandment?

The eighth commandment is, *Thou shalt not steal.*

76. Which is the ninth commandment?

The ninth commandment is, *Thou shalt not bear false witness against thy neighbor.*

79. Which is the tenth commandment?

The tenth commandment is, *Thou shalt not covet thy neighbor's house, thou shalt not covet thy neighbor's wife, nor his manservant, nor his maidservant, nor his ox, nor his ass, nor anything that is thy neighbor's.*

The Lord's Prayer

98. What is prayer?

Prayer is an offering up of our desires unto God, for things agreeable to his will, in the name of Christ, with confession of our sins, and thankful acknowledgment of his mercies.

99. What rule has God given for our direction in prayer?

The whole Word of God is of use to direct us in prayer; but the special rule of direction is that form of prayer which Christ taught his disciples, commonly called the Lord's Prayer.

100. What does the preface of the Lord's Prayer teach us?

The preface of the Lord's prayer, which is, *Our Father which art in heaven*, teaches us to draw near to God with all holy reverence and confidence, as children to a father able and ready to help us; and that we should pray with and for others.

101. What do we pray for in the first petition?

In the first petition, which is, *Hallowed be thy name*, we pray that God would enable us and others to glorify him in all that whereby he makes himself known; and that he would dispose all things to his own glory.

102. What do we pray for in the second petition?

In the second petition, which is, *Thy kingdom come*, we pray that Satan's kingdom may be destroyed; and that the kingdom of grace may be advanced, ourselves and others brought into it, and kept in it; and that the kingdom of glory may be hastened.

103. What do we pray for in the third petition?

In the third petition, which is, *Thy will be done in earth, as it is in heaven*, we pray that God, by his grace, would make us able and willing to know, obey, and submit to his will in all things, as the angels do in heaven.

104. What do we pray for in the fourth petition?

In the fourth petition, which is, *Give us this day our daily bread*, we pray that of God's free gift we may receive a competent portion of the good things of this life, and enjoy his blessing with them.

105. What do we pray for in the fifth petition?

In the fifth petition, which is, *And forgive us our debts, as we forgive our debtors*, we pray that God, for Christ's sake, would freely pardon all our sins; which we are the rather encouraged to ask, because by his grace we are enabled from the heart to forgive others.

106. What do we pray for in the sixth petition?

In the sixth petition, which is, *And lead us not into temptation, but deliver us from evil*, we pray that God would either keep us from being tempted to sin, or support and deliver us when we are tempted.

107. What does the conclusion of the Lord's Prayer teach us?

The conclusion of the Lord's Prayer, which is, *For thine is the kingdom, and the power, and the glory, forever, Amen*, teaches us to take our encouragement in prayer from God only, and in our prayers to praise him, ascribing kingdom, power, and glory to him. And in testimony of our desire, and assurance to be heard, we say, Amen.

SECOND GRADE

9. What is the work of creation?

The work of creation is God's making all things of nothing, by the word of his power, in the space of six days, and all very good.

10. How did God create man?

God created man male and female, after his own image, in knowledge, righteousness, and holiness, with dominion over the creatures.

11. What are God's works of providence?

God's works of providence are his most holy, wise, and powerful preserving and governing all his creatures, and all their actions.

12. What special act of providence did God exercise toward man in the estate wherein he was created?

When God had created man, he entered into a covenant of life with him, upon condition of perfect obedience; forbidding him to eat of the tree of the knowledge of good and evil, upon the pain of death.

13. Did our first parents continue in the estate wherein they were created?

Our first parents, being left to the freedom of their own will, fell from the estate wherein they were created, by sinning against God.

14. What is sin?

Sin is any want of conformity unto, or transgression of, the law of God.

15. What was the sin whereby our first parents fell from the estate wherein they were created?

The sin whereby our first parents fell from the estate wherein they were created was their eating the forbidden fruit.

16. Did all mankind fall in Adam's first transgression?

The covenant being made with Adam, not only for himself, but for his posterity; all mankind, descending from him by ordinary generation, sinned in him, and fell with him, in his first transgression.

17. Into what estate did the fall bring mankind?

The fall brought mankind into an estate of sin and misery.

18. Wherein consists the sinfulness of that estate whereinto man fell?

The sinfulness of that estate whereinto man fell consists in the guilt of Adam's first sin, the want of original righteousness, and the corruption of his whole nature, which is commonly called original sin; together with all actual transgressions which proceed from it.

19. What is the misery of that estate whereinto man fell?

All mankind by their fall lost communion with God, are under his wrath and curse, and so made liable to all miseries in this life, to death itself, and to the pains of hell forever.

20. Did God leave all mankind to perish in the estate of sin and misery?

God having, out of his mere good pleasure, from all eternity, elected some to everlasting life, did enter into a covenant of grace, to deliver them out of the estate of sin and misery, and to bring them into an estate of salvation by a redeemer.

21. Who is the redeemer of God's elect?

The only redeemer of God's elect is the Lord Jesus Christ, who, being the eternal Son of God, became man, and so was, and continues to be, God and man in two distinct natures, and one person, forever.

22. How did Christ, being the Son of God, become man?

Christ, the Son of God, became man, by taking to himself a true body and a reasonable soul, being conceived by the power of the Holy Ghost, in the womb of the virgin Mary, and born of her, yet without sin.

23. What offices does Christ execute as our redeemer?

Christ, as our redeemer, executes the offices of a prophet, of a priest, and of a king, both in his estate of humiliation and exaltation.

24. How does Christ execute the office of a prophet?

Christ executes the office of a prophet, in revealing to us, by his Word and Spirit, the will of God for our salvation.

25. How does Christ execute the office of a priest?

Christ executes the office of a priest, in his once offering up of himself a sacrifice to satisfy divine justice, and reconcile us to God; and in making continual intercession for us.

26. How does Christ execute the office of a king?

Christ executes the office of a king, in subduing us to himself, in ruling and defending us, and in restraining and conquering all his and our enemies.

27. Wherein did Christ's humiliation consist?

Christ's humiliation consisted in his being born, and that in a low condition, made under the law, undergoing the miseries of this life, the wrath of God, and the cursed death of the cross; in being buried, and continuing under the power of death for a time.

28. Wherein consisted Christ's exaltation?

Christ's exaltation consisted in his rising again from the dead on the third day, in ascending up into heaven, in sitting at the right hand of God the Father, and in coming to judge the world at the last day.

29. How are we made partakers of the redemption purchased by Christ?

We are made partakers of the redemption purchased by Christ, by the effectual application of it to us by his Holy Spirit.

30. How does the Spirit apply to us the redemption purchased by Christ?

The Spirit applies to us the redemption purchased by Christ, by working faith in us, and thereby uniting us to Christ in our effectual calling.

31. What is effectual calling?

Effectual calling is the work of God's Spirit, whereby, convincing us of our sin and misery, enlightening our minds in the knowledge of Christ, and renewing our wills, he does persuade and enable us to embrace Jesus Christ, freely offered to us in the gospel.

32. What benefits do they that are effectually called partake of in this life?

They that are effectually called do in this life partake of justification, adoption, and sanctification, and the several benefits which, in this life, do either accompany or flow from them.

33. What is justification?

Justification is an act of God's free grace, wherein he pardons all our sins, and accepts us as righteous in his sight, only for the righteousness of Christ imputed to us, and received by faith alone.

34. What is adoption?

Adoption is an act of God's free grace, whereby we are received into the number, and have a right to all the privileges of, the sons of God.

35. What is sanctification?

Sanctification is the work of God's free grace, whereby we are renewed in the whole man after the image of God, and are enabled more and more to die unto sin, and live unto righteousness.

THIRD GRADE

36. What are the benefits which in this life do accompany or flow from justification, adoption, and sanctification?

The benefits which in this life do accompany or flow from justification, adoption, and sanctification, are, assurance of God's love, peace of conscience, joy in the Holy Ghost, increase of grace, and perseverance therein to the end.

37. What benefits do believers receive from Christ at death?

The souls of believers are at their death made perfect in holiness, and do immediately pass into glory; and their bodies, being still united to Christ, do rest in their graves till the resurrection.

38. What benefits do believers receive from Christ at the resurrection?

At the resurrection, believers being raised up in glory, shall be openly acknowledged and acquitted in the day of judgment, and made perfectly blessed in the full enjoying of God to all eternity.

39. What is the duty which God requires of man?

The duty which God requires of man is obedience to his revealed will.

40. What did God at first reveal to man for the rule of his obedience?

The rule which God at first revealed to man for his obedience was the moral law.

41. Where is the moral law summarily comprehended?

The moral law is summarily comprehended in the Ten Commandments.

42. What is the sum of the Ten Commandments?

The sum of the Ten Commandments is to love the Lord our God with all our heart, with all our soul, with all our strength, and with all our mind; and our neighbor as ourselves.

43. What is the preface to the Ten Commandments?

The preface to the Ten Commandments is in these words, *I am the Lord thy God, which have brought thee out of the land of Egypt, out of the house of bondage.*

44. What does the preface to the Ten Commandments teach us?

The preface to the Ten Commandments teaches us that because God is the Lord, and our God, and redeemer, therefore we are bound to keep all his commandments.

82. Is any man able perfectly to keep the commandments of God?

No mere man since the fall is able in this life perfectly to keep the commandments of God, but does daily break them in thought, word, and deed.

83. Are all transgressions of the law equally heinous?

Some sins in themselves, and by reason of several aggravations, are more heinous in the sight of God than others.

84. What does every sin deserve?

Every sin deserves God's wrath and curse, both in this life, and that which is to come.

85. What does God require of us that we may escape his wrath and curse due to us for sin?

To escape the wrath and curse of God due to us for sin, God requires of us faith in Jesus Christ, repentance unto life, with the diligent use of all the outward means whereby Christ communicates to us the benefits of redemption.

86. What is faith in Jesus Christ?

Faith in Jesus Christ is a saving grace, whereby we receive and rest upon him alone for salvation, as he is offered to us in the gospel.

87. What is repentance unto life?

Repentance unto life is a saving grace, whereby a sinner, out of a true sense of his sin, and apprehension of the mercy of God in Christ, does, with grief and hatred of his sin, turn from it unto God, with full purpose of, and endeavor after, new obedience.

88. What are the outward and ordinary means whereby Christ communicates to us the benefits of redemption?

The outward and ordinary means whereby Christ communicates to us the benefits of redemption, are his ordinances, especially the Word, sacraments, and prayer; all which are made effectual to the elect for salvation.

89. How is the Word made effectual to salvation?

The Spirit of God makes the reading, but especially the preaching, of the Word, an effectual means of convincing and converting sinners, and of building them up in holiness and comfort, through faith, unto salvation.

90. How is the Word to be read and heard, that it may become effectual to salvation?

That the Word may become effectual to salvation, we must attend thereunto with diligence, preparation, and prayer; receive it with faith and love, lay it up in our hearts, and practice it in our lives.

91. How do the sacraments become effectual means of salvation?

The sacraments become effectual means of salvation, not from any virtue in them, or in him that does administer them; but only by the blessing of Christ, and the working of his Spirit in them that by faith receive them.

92. What is a sacrament?

A sacrament is a holy ordinance instituted by Christ; wherein, by sensible signs, Christ, and the benefits of the new covenant, are represented, sealed, and applied to believers.

93. Which are the sacraments of the New Testament?

The sacraments of the New Testament are baptism and the Lord's Supper.

94. What is baptism?

Baptism is a sacrament, wherein the washing with water in the name of the Father, and of the Son, and of the Holy Ghost, does signify and seal our ingrafting into Christ, and partaking of the benefits of the covenant of grace, and our engagement to be the Lord's.

95. To whom is baptism to be administered?

Baptism is not to be administered to any that are out of the visible church, till they profess their faith in Christ, and obedience to him; but the infants of such as are members of the visible church are to be baptized.

96. What is the Lord's Supper?

The Lord's Supper is a sacrament, wherein, by giving and receiving bread and wine according to Christ's appointment, his death is showed forth; and the worthy receivers are, not after a corporal and carnal manner, but by faith, made partakers of his body and blood, with all his benefits, to their spiritual nourishment and growth in grace.

97. What is required to the worthy receiving of the Lord's Supper?

It is required of them that would worthily partake of the Lord's Supper, that they examine themselves of their knowledge to discern the Lord's body, of their faith to feed upon him, of their repentance, love, and new obedience; lest, coming unworthily, they eat and drink judgment to themselves.

FOURTH GRADE

46. What is required in the first commandment?

The first commandment requires us to know and acknowledge God to be the only true God, and our God; and to worship and glorify him accordingly.

47. What is forbidden in the first commandment?

The first commandment forbids the denying, or not worshiping and glorifying the true God as God, and our God; and the giving of that worship and glory to any other, which is due to him alone.

48. What are we specially taught by these words *before me* in the first commandment?

These words *before me* in the first commandment teach us that God, who sees all things, takes notice of, and is much displeased with, the sin of having any other god.

50. What is required in the second commandment?

The second commandment requires the receiving, observing, and keeping pure and entire, all such religious worship and ordinances as God has appointed in his Word.

51. What is forbidden in the second commandment?

The second commandment forbids the worshiping of God by images, or any other way not appointed in his Word.

52. What are the reasons annexed to the second commandment?

The reasons annexed to the second commandment are, God's sovereignty over us, his propriety in us, and the zeal he has to his own worship.

54. What is required in the third commandment?

The third commandment requires the holy and reverent use of God's names, titles, attributes, ordinances, Word, and works.

55. What is forbidden in the third commandment?

The third commandment forbids all profaning or abusing of anything whereby God makes himself known.

56. What is the reason annexed to the third commandment?

The reason annexed to the third commandment is that however the breakers of this commandment may escape punishment from men, yet the Lord our God will not suffer them to escape his righteous judgment.

58. What is required in the fourth commandment?

The fourth commandment requires the keeping holy to God such set times as he has appointed in his Word; expressly one whole day in seven, to be a holy sabbath to himself.

59. Which day of the seven has God appointed to be the weekly sabbath?

From the beginning of the world to the resurrection of Christ, God appointed the seventh day of the week to be the weekly sabbath; and the first day of the week ever since, to continue to the end of the world, which is the Christian sabbath.

60. How is the sabbath to be sanctified?

The sabbath is to be sanctified by a holy resting all that day, even from such worldly employments and recreations as are lawful on other days; and spending the whole time in the public and private exercises of God's worship, except so much as is to be taken up in the works of necessity and mercy.

61. What is forbidden in the fourth commandment?

The fourth commandment forbids the omission or careless performance of the duties required, and the profaning the day by idleness, or doing that which is in itself sinful, or by unnecessary thoughts, words, or works, about our worldly employments or recreations.

62. What are the reasons annexed to the fourth commandment?

The reasons annexed to the fourth commandment are, God's allowing us six days of the week for our own employments, his challenging a special propriety in the seventh, his own example, and his blessing the sabbath day.

64. What is required in the fifth commandment?

The fifth commandment requires the preserving the honor, and performing the duties, belonging to every one in their several places and relations, as superiors, inferiors, or equals.

65. What is forbidden in the fifth commandment?

The fifth commandment forbids the neglecting of, or doing anything against, the honor and duty which belongs to every one in their several places and relations.

66. What is the reason annexed to the fifth commandment?

The reason annexed to the fifth commandment is a promise of long life and prosperity (as far as it shall serve for God's glory and their own good) to all such as keep this commandment.

68. What is required in the sixth commandment?

The sixth commandment requires all lawful endeavors to preserve our own life, and the life of others.

69. What is forbidden in the sixth commandment?

The sixth commandment forbids the taking away of our own life, or the life of our neighbor unjustly, or whatsoever tends thereunto.

71. What is required in the seventh commandment?

The seventh commandment requires the preservation of our own and our neighbor's chastity, in heart, speech, and behavior.

72. What is forbidden in the seventh commandment?

The seventh commandment forbids all unchaste thoughts, words, and actions.

74. What is required in the eighth commandment?

The eighth commandment requires the lawful procuring and furthering the wealth and outward estate of ourselves and others.

75. What is forbidden in the eighth commandment?

The eighth commandment forbids whatsoever does or may unjustly hinder our own or our neighbor's wealth or outward estate.

77. What is required in the ninth commandment?

The ninth commandment requires the maintaining and promoting of truth between man and man, and of our own and our neighbor's good name, especially in witness-bearing.

78. What is forbidden in the ninth commandment?

The ninth commandment forbids whatsoever is prejudicial to truth, or injurious to our own or our neighbor's good name.

80. What is required in the tenth commandment?

The tenth commandment requires full contentment with our own condition, with a right and charitable frame of spirit toward our neighbor, and all that is his.

81. What is forbidden in the tenth commandment?

The tenth commandment forbids all discontentment with our own estate, envying or grieving at the good of our neighbor, and all inordinate motions and affections to anything that is his.

REDEMPTIVE HISTORY
GRAMMAR

THE CORE OF HISTORY:

CREATION, FALL, REDEMPTION

An Outline of Redemptive History

I. In the Beginning

1. Creation: man is called to eternal life in knowing God

2. Fall: man chooses the way of sin and death

3. Redemption: man is called back by the curse and promise

II. From the Fall to the Flood

1. Universal Apostasy

2. Universal Judgment

3. The promise is preserved and renewed

III. From the Flood to Babel

1. Babel: uniting without God

2. Judgment: language divided and mankind scattered

3. The promise is preserved through one person for all mankind

IV. The Life and Times of the Patriarchs

1. The seed of Abraham

2. The seed of Isaac

3. The seed of Jacob

V. From Egypt to Canaan

1. The Exodus

2. The giving of the Law

3. Apostasy and wandering in the wilderness

VI. From Conquest to Kingship

1. The conquest of Canaan

2. Seven cycles of apostasy

3. From the priesthood to kingship

VII. From the Kings to Captivity

1. The life and times of the Kings

2. The prophets: call to repentance; the promise deepened

3. Judgment: the destruction of Israel and the exile of Judah

VIII. From the Exile to Christ

1. The Four Kingdoms

2. A remnant rebuilds

3. Apostasy and Judgment: tradition and foreign rule

IX. Christ in the Gospels

1. Christ revealed: his words and work

2. Christ rejected: crucified by the rulers

3. Christ reigning: resurrected and given all authority

X. Apostolic Christianity

1. Pentecost: the Church begins

2. Persecution: the Church grows

3. Apostolic writings: the Church established

XI. Early Church Fathers

1. Church Councils and Creeds

2. Gnosticism and Monasticism

3. The fall of Rome

XII. Medieval Christianity

1. Feudal Society

2. The Church: Scholasticism and Sacramentalism

3. The rise of Islam

XIII. The Reformation

1. Reformation Principles: The Five Solas

2. Religious wars

3. Tolerance of divisions

XIV. The Modern World

1. Age of discoveries

2. The Enlightenment

3. Expansion and World Wars

XV. The Post-Modern World

1. Secularism and Post-Christianity

2. Globalism and rivalry

3. The quest for unity: apostasy revisited or the promise?

8

TIMELINE OF

REDEMPTIVE HISTORY

15 Periods from Creation to the Present

8

I. In the Beginning (Genesis 1–3)

II. From the Fall to the Flood (2350 B.C.)

III. From the Flood to Babel (2240 B.C.)

IV. The Life and Times of the Patriarchs (2000–1640 B.C.)

V. From Egypt to Canaan (1485–1365 B.C.)

VI. From Conquest to Kingship (1365–1053 B.C.)

VII. From the Kings to Captivity (1053–536 B.C.)

VIII. From the Exile to Christ (536–4 B.C.)

IX. Christ in the Gospels (4 B.C.–A.D. 29)

X. Apostolic Christianity (A.D. 29–100)

XI. Early Church Fathers (A.D. 100–450)

XII. Medieval Christianity (A.D. 450–1500)

XIII. The Reformation (A.D. 1500–1648)

XIV. The Modern World (A.D. 1650–1950)

XV. The Post-Modern World (A.D. 1950–Present)

—

SCRIPTURE FOR MEMORIZATION

—

9

BIBLE VERSES
Grammar Clusters

CLARITY AND INEXCUSABILITY

Romans 1:18-20	Clarity and inexcusability
Romans 2:14-15	The law written on the heart
Deuteronomy 30:11-14	The law is in your mouth and in your heart
Psalm 19:1-6	The heavens declare the glory of God
Psalm 19:7-14	The law of the Lord is perfect
Isaiah 6:3	The whole earth is full of the glory of God

SIN AND DEATH

Romans 3:11; Psalm 14:2-3; 53:1-3	Definition of sin: no one seeks, no one understands, no one does what is right
Romans 3:23	All have sinned and fall short of the glory of God
Genesis 2:15-17	The day you eat of it you shall surely die
Romans 6:23	The wages of sin is spiritual death
Ephesians 2:1	Dead in transgressions and sins
John 11:25-26	Two kinds of life and death
Revelation 20:6, 14; 21:8	The second death is spiritual death
Romans 1:21-32	Progression of spiritual death

CURSE AND PROMISE

Genesis 3:14-19	Curse and promise
Psalm 90:7-12	Life under the curse
Genesis 12:1-3	The promise to Abraham
Genesis 22:7-8	God will provide the sacrifice
John 8:56	Abraham rejoiced at the thought
John 1:29	The Lamb of God

REPENTANCE AND FAITH

Genesis 3:20	Adam named his wife Eve
Hebrews 11:1-3, 6	Definition of faith
Ephesians 2:8-10	Salvation by faith alone
Hebrews 6:1-3	Repentance from dead works
Job 42:5-6	Now my eyes see you
Daniel 9:6-13	Turn from sin and understand thy truth
Jeremiah 9:23-24	Boast in knowing the Lord
Hebrews 11:4	By faith Abel sacrificed and through it he still speaks

JUSTIFICATION AND SANCTIFICATION

Genesis 3:21	Coats of skin
Romans 5:12, 16-19	Through the righteousness of the one
Galatians 2:16	Justified by faith in the Lord, not by the law
Galatians 3:8	Justification of the Gentiles by faith
John 17:17	Sanctification through the truth
John 8:31-32	The truth shall set us free
Psalm 51:4-13	Cleanse me in the inmost parts
Romans 12:1-3	Be transformed by the renewing of the mind
Psalm 27:4	One thing have I desired

Deuteronomy 6:4-9	Teach them diligently to your children
Genesis 3:22-24	Sanctification through suffering
Proverbs 3:11-12	The Lord corrects those he loves as a father
Luke 9:23	Pick up your cross daily
1 John 1:9	If we confess our sins
Matthew 13:23	Seed falling on good soil
Galatians 5:22-23	The fruit of the Spirit
Hebrews 12:1-3	Run with perseverance the race marked out for us

BAPTISM AND CALLING

John 3:3, 5-8	Regeneration by the Spirit
Romans 2:28-29	Circumcision of the heart
Colossians 2:11-12	Circumcised by Christ
1 Corinthians 12:12-13	Baptized in one body
Galatians 2:20	It is not I who lives, but Christ lives in me
Matthew 6:33	Seek first the kingdom
Ezekiel 36:26-27	I will give you a new heart
Hebrews 12:1-2	Run the race with perseverance

RESURRECTION AND REWARD

John 5:28-29	Physical resurrection
1 Corinthians 15:13-17	Argument for the resurrection
1 Corinthians 15:50-53	General resurrection
1 Corinthians 15:25-26	The last enemy is death
Revelation 21:3-5	Removal of the curse
1 Thessalonians 4:15-17	Resurrection of believer and unbeliever

SPIRITUAL WAR

Genesis 3:15	He will crush your head
2 Corinthians 10:4-5	Taking thoughts captive
Revelation 19:11-21	King of Kings and Lord of Lords
Ephesians 6:10-20	The armor of God
2 Timothy 2:23-26	Avoid foolish arguments
Matthew 7:6	Pearls before swine

ETERNAL LIFE/THE GOAL

John 17:3	Definition of eternal life
Genesis 1:26-28	The dominion/cultural mandate
Genesis 15:1	Our exceeding great reward
Philippians 3:7-8	The surpassing greatness of knowing Christ
1 Timothy 6:16	Knowledge of God is through his acts
Colossians 2:3	In Him are hidden all the treasures of wisdom
Isaiah 11:9	The earth shall be filled with the knowledge of the Lord

THE WORD OF GOD

John 1:1, 3-5, 10-11, 14, 18	The Logos
Isaiah 55:10-11	The Word will not return to Him void
Hebrews 4:12	The Word of God is alive and active
2 Timothy 3:16	The Word of God written
Hebrews 1:1-2	The Word of God making God known
Isaiah 40:8	The Word of the Lord endures forever

FOUNDATION

Hebrews 11:10	A city with foundations
Hebrews 5:11-14	By the time that you ought to be teachers
Hebrews 6:1-3	Let us go on to maturity
Matthew 7:24-27	The wise and foolish builder
1 Corinthians 3:10-15	As a wise master builder I have laid a foundation

THE CHURCH

1 Timothy 3:15	The Church is the pillar and foundation of the truth
Matthew 5:13-16	Salt and light
John 16:13	The Spirit will guide us into all truth
Psalm 48	The City of our God
1 Peter 2:9-10	A holy nation
Matthew 16:15-20	Upon this rock
Acts 1:8	Be witnesses unto the uttermost part of the earth

UNITY OF THE FAITH

Ephesians 4:11-16	Unity of the faith
John 17:20-23	Christ's high priestly prayer
1 Corinthians 1:13	Is Christ divided?

VICARIOUS ATONEMENT

John 1:29	The Lamb of God
Acts 26:22-23	The Messiah would suffer
Luke 24:25-26	Suffer then enter into glory
Isaiah 53:5-12	The suffering servant
Acts 4:12	*Solus Christus*

THE KINGDOM OF GOD

Luke 17:20-21	The kingdom of heaven is within you
Matthew 13:31-33	The parable of the mustard seed and yeast
Ezekiel 37:10-14	Can these bones live?
Matthew 28:18-20	The Great Commission

THE MORAL LAW

Exodus 20:3	First Commandment
Exodus 20:4-6	Second Commandment
Exodus 20:7	Third Commandment
Exodus 20:8-11	Fourth Commandment
Exodus 20:12	Fifth Commandment
Exodus 20:13	Sixth Commandment
Exodus 20:14	Seventh Commandment
Exodus 20:15	Eighth Commandment
Exodus 20:16	Ninth Commandment
Exodus 20:17	Tenth Commandment

THE CITY OF MAN

Colossians 2:8, 20	Hollow philosophy and elementary forces of this world
2 Peter 3:10, 12	The elements (*stoicheia*) will melt
Galatians 4:3, 9	Slavery to elemental spiritual forces
Jude 1:11	The way of Cain

THE FEAR OF THE LORD

Proverbs 1:7	The beginning of wisdom
Psalm 110:11	Obeying His commandments
Proverbs 19:23	The fear of the Lord leads to life

| Proverbs 14:2 | He who walks in uprightness fears the Lord |
| Proverbs 2:5 | The fear of the Lord and the knowledge of God |

THE LOVE OF GOD

John 3:16-21	For God so loved the world
Romans 5:8	While we were still sinners
Mark 12:29-31	The greatest commandment
1 John 5:2-4	To love God is to keep His commandments
Romans 8:35-36	Nothing can separate us from the love of God

CULPABLE IGNORANCE

Luke 23:34	Father, forgive them for they know not
John 16:2-3	Whoever kills you will think he is doing God's service
1 Timothy 1:13	Persecuted the Church ignorantly in unbelief
Acts 3:17	You and your rulers acted in ignorance
Hosea 4:6	My people are destroyed for lack of knowledge

ESCHATOLOGY

Psalm 2:5-12	I have set my king to reign
Psalm 22:27-31	All ends of earth will turn
Psalm 110	The session of Christ
Daniel 2:34-35, 44	The stone cut out without hands
Isaiah 2:1-5	The mountain of the Lord
Isaiah 4:4-6	The glory of the Lord shall be a defense
Isaiah 11:6-9	Renewed earth

Romans 8:19-23	Groaning for our adoption to sonship
Hebrews 11:39-40	The fullness of the blessing in unity
Revelation 21:1-2	The new Jerusalem coming down from heaven

PSALMS FOR SINGING[1]
Grammar Selection

Psalm 1A	Psalm 92A
Psalm 2	Psalm 100A
Psalm 8B	Psalm 104D
Psalm 15	Psalm 110
Psalm 19A	Psalm 119B
Psalm 19B	Psalm 119Q
Psalm 22I	Psalm 119M
Psalm 23B	Psalm 127A
Psalm 25C	Psalm 128B
Psalm 51D	Psalm 133A
Psalm 67A	Psalm 137
Psalm 78A	Psalm 148
Psalm 84B	Psalm 150B

---

1. *The Book of Psalms for Singing.* Pittsburgh, PA: Crown and Covenant.
See: crownandcovenant.com

SUGGESTED READING

PHILOSOPHICAL FOUNDATION

Philosophy:

Surrendra Gangadean, *Philosophical Foundation: A Critical Analysis of Basic Beliefs*

Surrendra Gangadean, *On Natural and Revealed Theology: Collected Essays of Surrendra Gangadean*

Peter Kreeft, *Socratic Logic: A Logic Text Using Socratic Method, Platonic Questions, and Aristotelian Principles*

Raymond McCall, *Basic Logic*

History of Philosophy:

Surrendra Gangadean, *History of Philosophy: A Critical Analysis of Unresolved Disputes*

Kelly Fitzsimmons Burton, *Retrieving Knowledge: A Socratic Response to Skepticism*

David K. Naugle, *Worldview: The History of a Concept*

Frederick Copleston, *The History of Philosophy* (11 Volumes)

Gordon H. Clark, *Thales to Dewey: A History of Philosophy*

Heinrich A. Rommen, *The Natural Law: A Study in Legal and Social History and Philosophy*

Stephen R. C. Hicks, *Explaining Postmodernism: Skepticism and Socialism from Rousseau to Foucault*

Susan Neiman, *Evil in Modern Thought: An Alternative History of Philosophy*

William Barrett, *Irrational Man: A Study in Existential Philosophy*

Worldview:

Albert Camus, *The Myth of Sisyphus*

Bernard Lewis, *The Crisis of Islam: Holy War and Unholy Terror*

Chandradhar Sharma, *A Critical Survey of Indian Philosophy*

Christian Smith, *The Secular Revolution: Power, Interests, and Conflict in the Secularization of American Public Life*

David Knowles, *The Evolution of Medieval Thought*

Eliot Deutsch, *Advaita Vedanta: A Philosophical Reconstruction*

Frederick Streng, *Emptiness: A Study in Religious Meaning*

Frederick W. Mote, *The Intellectual Foundations of China*

George M. Marsden, *The Soul of the American University: From Protestant Establishment to Established Nonbelief*

H. G. Creel, *Confucius and the Chinese Way*

Holmes H. Welch Jr., *Taoism: The Parting of the Way*

J.N.D. Anderson, *The World's Religions: Animism, Judaism, Islam, Hinduism, Buddhism, Shintoism, Confucianism*

Kenneth Cragg, *House of Islam* (The Religious Life of Man)

Mark A. Noll, *The Scandal of the Evangelical Mind*

Robert J. Collins, *The Vision of Buddhism: The Space Under the Tree*

Samuel Huntington, *The Clash of Civilizations and the Remaking of World Order*

Thomas Hopkins, *The Hindu Religious Tradition* (The Religious Life of Man)

Moral Law and Culture:

Allan Bloom, *The Closing of the American Mind: How Higher Education Has Failed Democracy and Impoverished the Souls of Today's Students*

Arnold Toynbee, *A Study of History: Abridgment of Volumes I-X* (2 Volumes)

Arthur C. Custance, *Noah's Three Sons: Human History in Three Dimensions* [The Doorway Papers]

Benjamin Wiker and Donald Demarco, *Architects of the Culture of Death*

Bernard Lewis, *What Went Wrong?: Western Impact and Middle Eastern Response*

C. S. Lewis, *The Abolition of Man*

Francis A. Schaeffer, *How Should We Then Live?: The Rise and Decline of Western Thought and Culture*

Gilbert Highet, *Paideia: The Ideals of Greek Culture* (3 Volumes)

Herbert Schlossberg, *Idols for Destruction: The Conflict of Christian Faith and American Culture*

Leland Ryken, *Worldly Saints: The Puritans as They Really Were*

Nancy Pearcey, *Total Truth: Liberating Christianity from Its Cultural Captivity*

Neil Postman: *Amusing Ourselves to Death: Public Discourse in the Age of Show Business*

Paul Johnson, *Intellectuals: From Marx and Tolstoy to Sartre and Chomsky*

Richard Hofstadter, *Anti-Intellectualism in American Life*

Robert H. Bork, *Slouching Towards Gomorrah: Modern Liberalism and American Decline*

Robert Reilly, *The Closing of the Muslim Mind: How Intellectual Suicide Created the Modern Islamic Crisis*

Rodney Stark, *The Victory of Reason: How Christianity Led to Freedom, Capitalism, and Western Success*

William Strauss and Neil Howe, *Generations: The History of America's Future 1584-2069*

William Strauss and Neil Howe, *The Fourth Turning: An American Prophecy*

Fourth Argument Against Materialism—Naturalism Is Not Based on Science:

Benjamin Wiker, *Moral Darwinism: How We Became Hedonists*

Cornelius G. Hunter, *Darwin's God: Evolution and The Problem of Evil*

Cornelius G. Hunter, *Darwin's Proof: The Triumph of Religion over Science*

Cornelius G. Hunter, *Science's Blind Spot: The Unseen Religion of Scientific Naturalism*

David Berlinski, *The Devil's Delusion: Atheism and Its Scientific Pretensions*

Dr. Russell Humphreys, *Starlight & Time: Solving the Puzzle of Distant Starlight in a Young Universe*

Henry M. Morris, *The Genesis Flood: The Biblical Record and its Scientific Implications*

John Horgan, *The End of Science: Facing the Limits of Knowledge in the Twilight of the Scientific Age*

Jonathan Wells, *The Icons of Evolution: Science or Myth? Why Much of What We Teach About Evolution Is Wrong*

Luther Sunderland, *Darwin's Enigma: Fossils and Other Problems*

Marvin L. Lubenow, *Bones of Contention: A Creationist Assessment of Human Fossils*

Philip E. Johnson, *Darwin on Trial*

Stephen C. Meyer, *Signature in the Cell: DNA and the Evidence for Intelligent Design*

Thomas Khun, *The Structure of Scientific Revolutions*

Walter T. Brown, *In the Beginning: Compelling Evidence for Creation and the Flood* (9th Edition)

William Lane Craig, *The Blackwell Companion to Natural Theology*

Economics:

Carl Menger, *Principles of Economics*

Frédéric Bastiat, *What Is Money?* (The Bastiat Collection)

Henry Hazlitt, *Economics in One Lesson: The Shortest and Surest Way to Understand Basic Economics*

Lawrence E. Harrison and Samuel P. Huntington, *Culture Matters: How Values Shape Human Progress*

Ludwig von Mises, *Human Action, The Scholar's Edition*

Murray N. Rothbard, *An Austrian Perspective on the History of Economic Thought* (2 Volumes)

Robert L. Heilbroner, *The Worldly Philosophers: The Lives, Times and Ideas of the Great Economic Thinkers*

THEOLOGICAL FOUNDATION

Theology:

Surrendra Gangadean, *Theological Foundation: A Critical Analysis of Christian Belief*

Surrendra Gangadean, *The Logos Papers: To Make the Logos Known*

Surrendra Gangadean, *The Biblical Worldview: Creation, Fall, Redemption Genesis 1–3: Scripture in Organic Seed Form*

Surrendra Gangadean, *The Book of Job: Deepening the Revelation of God's Glory for All Time—An Ironic Theodicy*

Surrendra Gangadean, *The Book of Revelation: What Must Soon Take Place—Doxological Postmillennialism*

Surrendra Gangadean, *The Epistle to the Romans: The Righteousness of God Revealed from Faith to Faith—The Gospel According to St. Paul*

Alexander Hislop, *The Two Babylons: Or, the Papal Worship Proved to Be the Worship of Nimrod*

Alfred Edersheim, *The Life and Times of Jesus the Messiah: Complete and Unabridged in One Volume*

Anthony A. Hoekema, *The Four Major Cults: Christian Science, Jehovah's Witnesses, Mormonism, Seventh-day Adventism*

Archibald Alexander, *The Evidences of the Christian Religion* (Introduction)

Benjamin B. Warfield, *Counterfeit Miracles: A History of Fake Miracles and Healings in the Christian and Catholic Traditions, with Arguments in Favor of Cessationism*

C. S. Lewis, *The Great Divorce*

Charles Hodge, *Systematic Theology* (3 Volumes)

Douglas Groothuis, *Christian Apologetics: A Comprehensive Case for Biblical Faith*

Francis A. Schaeffer, *The Francis A. Schaeffer Trilogy: Three Essential Books in One Volume (The God Who Is There; Escape From Reason; He Is There And He Is Not Silent)*

Iain H. Murray, *The Puritan Hope: Revival and the Reinterpretation of Prophecy*

J. P. Moreland, *Love Your God with All Your Mind: The Role of Reason in the Life of the Soul*

Joel R. Beeke and Randall J. Pederson, *Meet the Puritans: With a Guide to Modern Reprints*

Kenneth Boa, *Faith Has Its Reasons: Integrative Approaches to Defending the Christian Faith*

Lorainne Boettner, *The Millennium*

Lorainne Boettner, *The Reformed Doctrine of Predestination*

Marcellus Kik, *An Eschatology of Victory*

Michael Bushell, *Songs of Zion: The Biblical Basis for Exclusive Psalmody*

O. Palmer Robertson, *The Christ of the Covenants*

O. Palmer Robertson, *The Christ of the Prophets: Abridged Edition*

O. Palmer Robertson, *The Final Word: A Biblical Response to the Case for Tongues and Prophecy Today*

R. C. Sproul, J. Gerstner, and A. Lindsley, *Classical Apologetics: A Rational Defense of the Christian Faith and a Critique of Presuppositional Apologetics*

Søren Kierkegaard, *Fear and Trembling*

Søren Kierkegaard, *Purity of Heart Is To Will One Thing*

W. J. Conybeare, *The Life and Epistles of St. Paul*

HISTORICAL FOUNDATION

Church History:

Surrendra Gangadean, *The Westminster Confession of Faith: A Doxological Understanding*

Surrendra Gangadean, *The Westminster Shorter and Larger Catechisms: A Doxological Understanding*

Benjamin B. Warfield, *The Works of Benjamin B. Warfield: Volume 6—The Westminster Assembly and Its Work*

Etienne Gilson, *Reason and Revelation in the Middle Ages*

James C. Livingston, *Modern Christian Thought* (2 Volumes)

Justo L. Gonzalez, *A History of Christian Thought* (3 Volumes)

Justo L. Gonzalez, *The Story of Christianity: The Early Church to the Present Day*

Philip Schaff, *History of the Christian Church* (8 Volumes)